The Family:
A World History

The New
Oxford
World
History

The Family:
A World History

Mary Jo Maynes and Ann Waltner

OXFORD

UNIVERSITY PRESS

OXFORD
UNIVERSITY PRESS

Oxford University Press, Inc., publishes works that further
Oxford University's objective of excellence
in research, scholarship, and education.

Oxford   New York
Auckland   Cape Town   Dar es Salaam   Hong Kong   Karachi
Kuala Lumpur   Madrid   Melbourne   Mexico City   Nairobi
New Delhi   Shanghai   Taipei   Toronto

With offices in
Argentina   Austria   Brazil   Chile   Czech Republic   France   Greece
Guatemala   Hungary   Italy   Japan Poland   Portugal   Singapore
South Korea   Switzerland   Thailand   Turkey   Ukraine   Vietnam

Library of Congress Cataloging-in-Publication Data
The family : a world history / by Mary Jo Maynes and Ann Waltner.
p. cm. — (New Oxford world history)
Includes bibliographical references and index.
ISBN 978-0-19-533814-0 (pbk. : alk. paper) — ISBN 978-0-19-530476-3 (hbk. : alk. paper)
1. Families—History. I. Waltner, Ann Beth. II. Title.
HQ503.M327   2012
306.85—dc23   2011046814

1 3 5 7 9 8 6 4 2
Printed in the United States of America
on acid-free paper
Frontispiece: A nineteenth-century British illustration of the presentation of the
Christmas pudding. *Fine Art Photographic Library, London /Art Resource, NY*

Contents

Editors' Preface

This book is part of the New Oxford World History, an innovative series that offers readers an informed, lively, and up-to-date history of the world and its people that represents a significant change from the "old" world history. Only a few years ago, world history generally amounted to a history of the West—Europe and the United States—with small amounts of information from the rest of the world. Some versions of the "old" world history drew attention to every part of the world *except* Europe and the United States. Readers of that kind of world history could get the impression that somehow the rest of the world was made up of exotic people who had strange customs and spoke difficult languages. Still another kind of "old" world history presented the story of areas or peoples of the world by focusing primarily on the achievements of great civilizations. One learned of great buildings, influential world religions, and mighty rulers but little of ordinary people or more general economic and social patterns. Interactions among the world's peoples were often told from only one perspective.

This series tells world history differently. First, it is comprehensive, covering all countries and regions of the world and investigating the total human experience—even those of so-called peoples without histories living far from the great civilizations. "New" world historians thus share in common an interest in all of human history, even going back millions of years before there were written human records. A few "new" world histories even extend their focus to the entire universe, a "big history" perspective that dramatically shifts the beginning of the story back to the big bang. Some see the "new" global framework of world history today as viewing the world from the vantage point of the Moon, as one scholar put it. We agree. But we also want to take a close-up view, analyzing and reconstructing the significant experiences of all of humanity.

This is not to say that everything that has happened everywhere and in all time periods can be recovered or is worth knowing, but that there is much to be gained by considering both the separate and interrelated stories of different societies and cultures. Making these connections is still another crucial ingredient of the "new" world history. It emphasizes connectedness and interactions of all kinds—cultural, economic, political, religious, and social—involving peoples, places, and processes. It makes comparisons and finds similarities. Emphasizing both the comparisons and interactions is critical to developing a global framework that can deepen and broaden historical understanding, whether the focus is on a specific country or region or on the whole world.

The rise of the new world history as a discipline comes at an opportune time. The interest in world history in schools and among the general public is vast. We travel to one another's nations, converse and work with people around the world, and are changed by global events. War and peace affect populations worldwide as do economic conditions and the state of our environment, communications, and health and medicine. The New Oxford World History presents local histories in a global context and gives an overview of world events seen through the eyes of ordinary people. This combination of the local and the global further defines the new world history. Understanding the workings of global and local conditions in the past gives us tools for examining our own world and for envisioning the interconnected future that is in the making.

Bonnie G. Smith
Anand Yang

Preface

People have always lived in families, but what that means has changed dramatically over time. The family is a historical institution, not a natural one. Families both have a history and make history. This is the starting point for this book, which looks at family history across cultures and over a very long span of time, since 10,000 BCE. We do not aim for comprehensive coverage (which would be sheer folly even in a very long book); rather, our goal is to address the question of how world history looks when the family is at the center of the story.

There are two ways in which we place the family at the center of history, ways that are related but are not identical. We take the family and its variation over time and place as our focus; that is, we look, for example, at childbearing patterns, or gender division of labor, or mate selection—all dimensions of family life in particular times and places. We explore how these aspects of family life change over time, and how different cultures have found their own specific ways of organizing family life. That is, we show that the family as a social institution has a history; that families are not natural or unchanging entities that remain the same over time and across cultures.

For example, in some times and places, men have had more than one wife at a time; in some times and places, married children have usually lived with the parents of one of the spouses; in many times and places, marriage partners have been selected by the parents of the marrying couple. All of these practices seemed normal and ordinary to the people who engaged in them; by looking at a wide variety of practices we can see how none of them (including our own family practices) are "natural"—they are all socially and historically constructed. In this book, we will look both at stability and change over time, at similarities and variations across cultures in how families work. Thus, one of the things we mean when we put the family at the center of history is that family structures change over time and that those changes are related in historically significant ways to social and political and cultural processes.

But families are also agents of historical change, and households are sites of history. For example, children are socialized within family groups. It is within the family that one first learns how to be a twenty-first-century

American or learned how to be a sixteenth-century Chinese; family socialization is key to the construction of cultural or national identities. Cultural capital and religious values are also transmitted within families; families shape individual and collective predispositions and destinies. Arrangements made by and within families (such as marriage choices, or bequests of property, or decisions about educating children) contribute to social dynamism or stability, alongside and sometimes even more powerfully than economic systems, government policies, or intellectual movements.

Power itself, often thought to occupy a realm of "public" life distinct from the domestic realm of the family, nevertheless can rarely be understood without reference to family in a literal or a metaphoric sense. For example, royal power is passed through family lines in dynastic systems, but even in formal democracies influential families often wield power through election. Even where there are no dynasties of either sort, family metaphors such as "the brotherhood of man" or "our founding fathers" hold tremendous influence over political thought.

In other realms, merchant or corporate elite families use kin networks to build and organize long-distance trade or to further business interests. Migration streams rely on familial networks as well as economic magnetism, and so on. When one looks at politics, economics, or migration this way, families emerge as agents of historical transformation, not just as its object.

Before we embark on this kind of history, we need to specify what we mean by family. For our purposes here, a very general and inclusive definition of family is useful: families are small groups of people linked by culturally recognized ties of marriage or similar forms of partnership, descent, and/or adoption, who typically share a household for some period of time. This coresidence is necessarily temporary and varies over the stages of the family cycle. Families are thus not identical to households. Family members do not always share a residence. Ties of kinship are not broken simply because someone moves out of the family home, though the nature of the relationship might change as, for example, a daughter moves to her new husband's household, or a son goes off to apprentice at a cousin's shop, or a child is sold into slavery. Nor is coresidence always a sign of kinship.

There are also numerous arrangements where people who are not related to one another share a household—roommates, apprentices, and servants are examples of types of people who share a household but are not related to one another and do not consider each other as family. Thus, the history of the family is connected to the history of the household, but it is not the same. Different societies have different definitions of who counts as family members; in some societies your mother's second cousin is a kinsman of note, while in others (such as our own) many people cannot even name their mother's second cousins. To study the ways in which societies account for their own kinship relations, we in general adopt an expansive and inclusive definition of family—if the people we are looking at regarded themselves as related, we do too.

Although it may seem that the time span of this book is ambitious, in fact it is the tip of the iceberg of global history in the broadest terms. Increasingly, historians have become interested in "big history," which posits time frames in the context of geological history—a true history of the globe since the earth's beginning. Even short of this immense geological time span, other historians argue for the need to understand episodes of human development that occurred millennia before the appearance of the earliest of the written records so dear to the traditional craft of history.[1] Taking a long view brings to light processes of human development and patterns of social life that elude investigations limited to shorter time spans.

To use a spatial metaphor to help us think about time, writing a history of the family beginning in 10,000 BCE provides a big picture—a sort of aerial photo—from which to consider more detailed periods and more particular stories. The long temporal framework enables us to see broad contours, even as it obscures details. But deep history also provides us with methodological insights. Thinking about the material evidence that is the mainstay for archaeologists who examine "prehistoric" epochs gives us new insights about what similar material evidence can tell us about more recent epochs, where there is more ample textual documentation. Such evidence is particularly interesting, for example, for investigating the household as a site of ongoing human development and domestic activities as engines that have driven human history since its very origins. This book, focusing on the family in particular, is in this way also engaged in a wider conversation about deep history, what it means to be human, and how a very expansive temporal frame of world history brings to light new patterns and new insights into the human past and present.

CHAPTER I

Domestic Life and Human Origins (to 5000 BCE)

Archaeologists have found female figurines that seem to emphasize procreation at sites of Eurasian settlement dating from the thirtieth through the fourth millennium BCE. Some scholars have seen this as evidence of an ancient widespread religious cult based on a mother goddess; even though this specific claim has not been proven, the popularity of these figurines emphasizes the symbolic centrality of mother figures in early human cultures.[1]

Material evidence (including figures, but also dwellings and implements) for the earliest human societies continues to be uncovered, and the scientific tools to interpret that evidence are constantly being refined. As a result, historical and archaeological theories about family and gender relations in early human society have varied over time. One of Europe's first practicing archaeologists, the nineteenth-century German scholar Johann Bachofen, hypothesized that the earliest human social groupings were sexually promiscuous, but that soon order was imposed when matriarchal, or mother-dominated, societies created the first recognizable human cultures. Only later in human evolution, in Bachofen's view, did patriarchal (that is, father- or male-dominated) forms of household and society displace the primitive "rule of the mother."[2]

These nineteenth-century claims about the significance of mothers and domestic life for early human civilization were largely forgotten in the twentieth century as Western scholars turned to explanations of the origins of human society that focused on "Man the Hunter." Up through the early 1980s, the predominant claim among scientists was that men's hunting activities brought about the technological discoveries and the impulse for social organization that led to the development of early human cultures. Men, according to this line of thought, competed with each other for mates and supplied food for their mates and their children; this division of labor supposedly allowed women to focus on bearing and nurturing offspring. In this picture, women, and

These two baked clay female figures, dating from the sixth millennium BCE, *were found in what is now northern Syria. Figures like this are commonly found at sites of early human settlement in Eurasia, suggesting connections between early ritual practices and human fertility, symbolized by the figures' enlarged breasts.* Erich Lessing /Art Resource, NY

domestic life more generally, played at most a passive role in human evolution, largely restricted to reproduction, understood primarily in biological rather than cultural terms.

Beginning in the 1980s, new ways of thinking about gender, propelled by feminist scholarship combined with new forms of evidence and new ways of analyzing it, prompted still another revision. The debates continue, and although there is not yet a consensus, recent scholarship challenges the view of early human culture as the product of primarily masculine activities even as it rejects the notion of a primitive matriarchy.

Some of the newer evidence comes from primatology; studies of chimpanzees (our closest primate relatives) show that females are not dependent on males for food and that female chimps are inventive tool makers. Moreover, evidence about hunter-gatherer societies (both contemporary and ancient) suggests that the diets of hunter-gatherers can be quite diverse—large game meat is by no means the only food consumed, and women's foraging can provide a high proportion of a group's nutritional needs. Analogies from contemporary hunter-gatherer societies (not to mention those derived from other species) must of course be applied with great caution in historical arguments, but they form pieces of an evidential puzzle that allow us to think about early human societies in new and productive ways.

Groups with genetic traits similar to modern humans have been around for hundreds of thousands of years. Our close relatives first appeared in East Africa over two million years ago. Archaeological evidence from some of the earliest sites of human settlement in East Africa and elsewhere do in fact show that early foraging societies relied on a variety of foodstuffs. The findings now suggest that kinship and family relations played a prominent role in the acquiring and sharing of food, and thus in the evolution of human society, from the very start.

Foraging groups were quite mobile; evidence about the location of camps and food and bone residues suggests that both men and women were on the move. Objects found in preagricultural societies in East Africa, for example, might indicate that men and women moved out from and returned periodically to places where they shared the bounty of hunting and foraging with each other. The mixing in one location of animal bones, the products of the hunt, and shards of pottery associated with foraging and pastoral groups may even suggest intermarriages among subgroups that fitted themselves in different ways to East Africa's ecology.[3] Early human societies did rely on some form of division of labor between men and women, but these involved women in both production (especially foraging for food) and reproduction. Moreover, it seems likely that the most persistent social unit was the mother-offspring unit rather than a male-dominated household based on a heterosexual bond. Bachofen's claim that "mother-rule" typified the era of the emergence of human civilizations may not be fully justified, but there is ample evidence that women played a very active role in supporting themselves and their offspring and organizing group life.

The quest for food has been at the core of each of the various patterns through which complex human cultures emerged, beginning around 10,000 years ago. The main modes of subsistence have been hunting and gathering (that is, reliance on a diet based mainly on undomesticated animal and plant foods), pastoralism (a diet based mainly on herds of domesticated animals), and agriculture (a diet based mainly on domesticated animals and plants). Beginning at the end of the last Ice Age, around 10,000 BCE or a bit earlier, human groups started to build permanent structures and settlements and to practice agriculture. The other main sources of livelihood, generally entailing nomadic or seminomadic styles of life, coexisted in many world regions; even where settlement agriculture was practiced, they existed as a supplement to cultivation. The history of family roles and relationships is closely connected to these various modes of acquiring foodstuffs.

For a long time, Western scholars assumed that agriculture was first practiced in an area of the Middle East known as the Fertile Crescent around 10,000 BCE. The precise process leading to this momentous change in this region is difficult to pin down. The most plausible story goes as follows: foragers who gathered and stored grasses and other plants to feed themselves and their animals probably noticed that some of the seeds on the plant stalks sprouted and grew near their storage places. The accidental production of "crops" could, over the course of time, be adopted as a permanent strategy for supplementing and eventually supplanting foraging.[4]

But agriculture was also invented in places other than the Fertile Crescent. According to recent archaeological findings there is now evidence for at least ten centers of origin of plant domestication, including Africa, southern India, and New Guinea. Domestication did not mean an instant transformation in the ways in which people obtained their food; in many regions, people seem to have experimented with farming to supplement their diet while continuing hunting and gathering activities.[5]

Farming was associated with a variety of other important innovations as, for example, pottery and basketry skills that had been developed earlier now became useful to make vessels needed to store crops. Kilns used for pottery making encouraged the development of metalworking technologies in some regions, which in turn made it possible to produce variations in agricultural implements such as metal plows. All of these innovations involved new household divisions of labor as new tasks were gradually introduced and old ones disappeared.

The introduction of agriculture has long been viewed as a great step forward for human development and has been written into basic concepts of historical evolution such as the "Neolithic Revolution," referring to a complex of changes brought about by the adoption of agriculture. Certainly agriculture marked a transition toward a world more recognizable to modern humans; it permitted many more people to live continuously in a given area, and was crucial to the growth of larger and denser settlements and thus to the emergence of more complex societies.[6]

But agricultural modes of life also brought new problems. Agriculture and the domestication of animals drastically altered ecologies. Skeletal remains suggest that early agricultural societies were more prone to disease than roughly contemporaneous hunter-gatherer societies. Domesticated animals transmitted new diseases to farming populations. Denser settlements of humans facilitated the spread of disease within communities. Under primitive technological conditions, agriculture was prone to failures that could lead to famine. The skeletons of European farmers of the late Stone Age were of shorter stature than the hunter-gatherers who preceded them, suggesting that as population increased with farming, individuals on the average may have had a less nourishing diet than their hunter-gatherer ancestors.[7] The cause and effect here are not entirely clear; societies may have begun the practice of sedentary agriculture only when hunting and gathering ceased to be viable options because of population growth or the depletion of resources.

Moreover, agriculture is more labor-intensive than hunting and gathering. Agriculture most likely meant more daily hours of labor for both men and women, although there is variation among early agricultural societies in how these changes played out.

The transition to agriculture and its more settled lifestyle brought a major reorganization of household labor patterns, task specialization, and domestic life more broadly.[8] In some areas, task specialization meant that women could center more of their subsistence work close to the settlements even while men in their kinship networks still roamed as hunters. For example, evidence about food production in the valley of the Nile dating from around the ninth millennium BCE associates women in particular with the more sedentary "new" pursuits like agriculture and pottery making; the location of tools and other objects associated with women's tasks suggest they were becoming less geographically mobile than men.

In West Africa, where sparse populations made hunting and gathering practicable for far longer, similar spatial distribution evidence from Kintampo in contemporary Ghana suggests that beginning around 4000 BCE women established more or less permanent home camps with their children while men of their kin groups continued to roam to hunt.

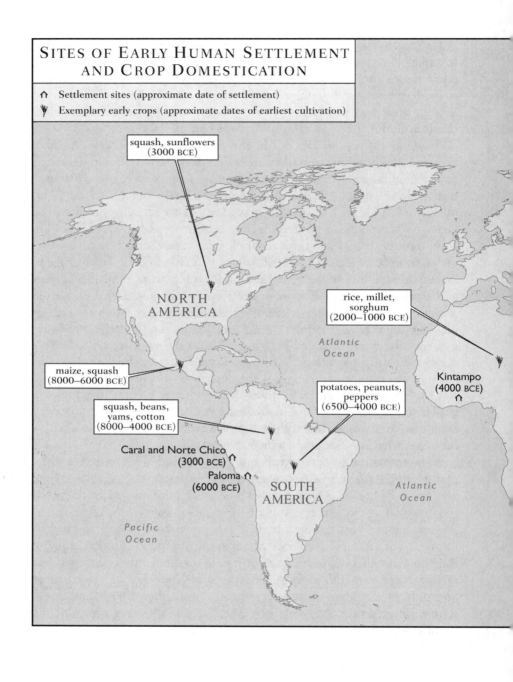

SITES OF EARLY HUMAN SETTLEMENT AND CROP DOMESTICATION

⇧ Settlement sites (approximate date of settlement)
🌾 Exemplary early crops (approximate dates of earliest cultivation)

squash, sunflowers
(3000 BCE)

NORTH
AMERICA

rice, millet,
sorghum
(2000–1000 BCE)

Atlantic
Ocean

maize, squash
(8000–6000 BCE)

Kintampo
(4000 BCE)
⇧

potatoes, peanuts,
peppers
(6500–4000 BCE)

squash, beans,
yams, cotton
(8000–4000 BCE)

Caral and Norte Chico
(3000 BCE) ⇧

Paloma ⇧
(6000 BCE)

SOUTH
AMERICA

Atlantic
Ocean

Pacific
Ocean

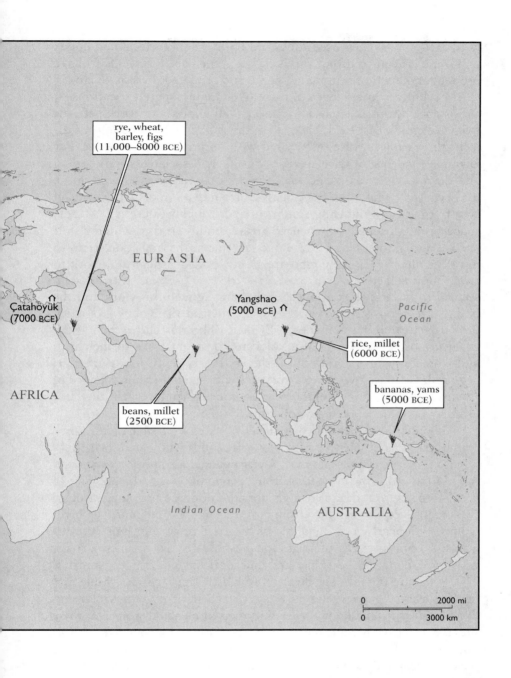

rye, wheat,
barley, figs
(11,000–8000 BCE)

EURASIA

Çatahöyük
(7000 BCE)

Yangshao
(5000 BCE)

Pacific
Ocean

rice, millet
(6000 BCE)

AFRICA

beans, millet
(2500 BCE)

bananas, yams
(5000 BCE)

Indian Ocean

AUSTRALIA

0   2000 mi
0   3000 km

Both men and women used tools and both produced food and goods that were crucial to group survival, but settlement life seems to have brought about a more emphatic spatial and gendered division of labor.[9]

In addition to evidence about the changing spatial locations of subsistence activities, archaeologists can tell a lot about work patterns from skeletal bones. Evidence of joint diseases and deformations document the various stresses associated with different types of work. For example, evidence of knee arthritis was likely associated with kneeling and digging, whereas particular shoulder or wrist stresses were more likely caused by hunting. Bone analyses from two Illinois settlements in North America of the Late Archaic period (roughly 3000 to 1000 BCE) suggest that all people experienced greater bodily stresses with the shift toward agriculture. However, in one settlement, the transition seems to have been harder on men, who apparently added agricultural work to their hunting activities; in another settlement, it was women who seemed to have taken on much of the new agricultural work and the bodily stresses associated with it, while men in their networks stuck primarily to hunting activities.[10] Evidence like this shows that small groups, most likely kin groups, allocated different tasks to their men and women members and pooled the various types of foodstuffs thus acquired. Changes over time associated with the increasing reliance of resource-pooling households on agriculture therefore left different imprints on male and female skeletons.

Although the evidence is very sketchy, it seems possible that in some regions patterns of intermarriage between groups who based their livelihoods on different ecologies may have facilitated a transition to agriculture. In East African sites dating from around 5000 BCE, the presence of pottery goods from distant regions provides evidence of complementary cross-marriages between men from pastoral cultures and hunter-gatherer women.[11] Similarly, bone analysis of Bronze Age sites in Italy suggests gender-specific patterns of migration possibly related to intermarriage between male farmers seeking land and local hunter-gatherer women.[12] This is demonstrated, once again, through skeletal analyses. Male and female skeletons at these sites show different chemical make-ups related to different diets in childhood. Over time, diets of men and women at these sites seem to have become more similar as a result of a completed transition to agriculture; this contrasts with the earlier pattern marked in the bones of men and women whose childhoods had been spent in different food environments.

At Çatalhöyük, in what is now Turkey, archaeologists have excavated an unusually well-preserved early agricultural settlement dating from around 7000 BCE. Çatalhöyük is the oldest known human settlement of significant size—around 9,000 years ago, between 3,000 and 8,000 people lived there. The people of Çatalhöyük engaged primarily in subsistence agriculture—they grew cereals and legumes, raised sheep and goats, and hunted some wild cattle—but the presence of dates, shells, and obsidian suggests some long-distance trade.

Because of the unusually high level of preservation of structures and of the artifacts of everyday and ritual life, this site is important for understanding the dynamics of an early agricultural society. In Çatalhöyük, kinship and household life served as the basis of social organization of the agricultural settlement. The settlement site contains a large number of buildings clustered in two large mounds and spread over fourteen levels. The levels were created as people tore down old houses, filled them in, and built new ones on top. Each building housed five to ten people. According to the archaeologists who have studied the site, a typical house had two rooms with specific areas for functions related to everyday activities, like cooking and crafts, but also for ritual life and the burial of dead family members.[13]

Contradicting the usual association in ancient history narratives between complex social organization and centralized political authority, Çatalhöyük seems to have been a community where social life was organized at the domestic, or household, scale. There is no evidence of public spaces, administrative buildings, or even unusually large or elaborate homes or quarters. There were few or no streets; people entered and left the houses by means of ladders that led to the rooftops. Complex economic and ritual functions, including the production of implements and the rites of burial, took place in individual households, along with the more predictable food preparation and child rearing. The buildings were richly decorated with sculptures such as fertility figurines and painted with murals, which suggests that these domestic spaces were also ritual spaces. Despite the town's relatively large size and complexity, the kin-based household seems to have been the primary social unit. All of the essential practices of this society seem to have been organized at the household level.

Archaeologists can deduce from the evidence in these buildings a great deal about the everyday life of various family members, including children. Children would have observed which domestic areas were for the living and which for the ancestors buried in special areas of the house. They would see adults making objects like beads or statues and learn by watching them. They would learn how to perform rituals and how to build or repair the house itself.

Kin relations may even account for Çatalhöyük's spatial layout. There are hints that the people of Çatalhöyük were divided into two groups who lived on opposite sides of the town, separated by a gully. Since there were no nearby towns from which marriage partners could be drawn, this spatial separation may have marked two intermarrying kinship groups. Moreover, the growing importance of kin links in agricultural societies may help to explain why a settlement complex as large as Çatalhöyük evolved in the first place. By living close together in the densely settled community, people built up associations with the domestic spaces and with each other that lasted over generations. Households could look to neighbors nearby for help, for trade, and for marriage partners for their children.

It is fair to say that in this early agricultural settlement human culture was based on household life and emerged out of domestic spaces. Social, political, economic, and even ritual relationships evolved in this elaborated domestic milieu and depended on the gender, generational, and kinship relations rooted in everyday life. Other early agricultural settlements vary in the particulars, but all offer evidence of the importance of household and family ties in this key transition in early human history.

The spatial organization of the Yangshao culture in North China was quite different from that of Çatalhöyük. The Yangshao culture (5000–3000 BCE) centered on a series of small agricultural villages along the Yellow, Wei, and Fen rivers and their tributaries. While people of Yangshao practiced slash-and-burn agriculture, a number of sites were reoccupied over time, indicating a practice of returning to previously inhabited places. Yangshao farmers grew millet, wheat, and rice, and domesticated animals such as pigs. A typical Yangshao village was laid out with houses arranged in clusters around a central plaza and pottery kilns and graveyards a small distance away from the center. The housing clusters may have been organized by kin group. We can imagine that a child in a Yangshao village would have learned which spaces were domestic, which were associated with the kin group, and which were more general public spaces. In addition, a female child probably learned that when she married, she would leave the village—a DNA analysis of skeletal remains suggests that women in Yangshao villages married out. These marriages may have provided connections among Yangshao villages.[14]

Men and women in Yangshao villages performed different sorts of labor, and these differences are reflected in the archaeological record. Agricultural tools (such as hoes and plows) and grinding tools are normally not found in the same graves, nor are agricultural tools normally

This artist's drawing illustrates the general layout of a Yangshao village (5000–3000 BCE), near present day Xi'an in China. The village is surrounded by a moat. Archaeological analysis shows that the clusters of dwellings within the village were home to specific kin groups. From Xiaoneng Yang, *New Perspectives on China's Past: Chinese Archaeology in the Twentieth Century,* Yale University Press and Nelson-Atkins Museum of Art, 2004, 103. Used with permission.

found in the same graves as spinning whorls. In sites where analyses have confirmed the gender of the occupants of graves, spinning whorls are found primarily in the graves of women and stone axes are found primarily in the graves of men.[15] In early Yangshao, goods tend to be fairly equally distributed among graves in a particular cemetery. In later periods, there is a greater degree of differentiation in the lavishness of burials, and men in general were more lavishly buried than were women. This may suggest a decline in the status of women and growing contrasts over time between people with wealth and power and those without.

As in Çatalhöyük, Yangshao graveyards suggest the significance of relations with the dead. In some of the cemeteries, small pits containing ash remains indicate that rituals were performed at the graves. A number of the graves that have been excavated contain numerous bodies, with bones arranged in ways that suggest that the bodies had been reburied; for example, the skulls had been placed in the center of the grave with other bones placed on both sides of the skulls. These reburials suggest an important ritual treatment of the dead, perhaps indicating the transformation of the dead into ancestors. Many more of the reburied skeletons are male, indicating that men were more likely to have been venerated as ancestors than women. It is noteworthy, however, that some women did indeed receive the rituals of reburial and hence attained the status of ancestress. It is also noteworthy that ancestor veneration on the north

China plain, as in Turkey, seems to have preceded any large state structure. In Yangshao, as in Çatalhöyük, social complexity emerged from the domestic and the local.[16]

We see a somewhat different pattern in the New World's oldest sites of human settlement, along the Peruvian coast. Excavations done at the coastal site of Paloma, which was occupied between 6000 and 3000 BCE, reveal that households were the basic unit of production, consumption, and ritual, even though we do see more evidence than in the other two cases of specialized political organization. Storage pits at the site are located near houses, and it appears that men, women, and children were buried underneath still-occupied houses. The settlements in Paloma were small, and connections between settlements were forged by marriage connections. In about the fourth millennium BCE, inland communities began to practice horticulture in "fog oases"—areas where fog provided much-needed moisture in otherwise arid regions—first growing gourds and cotton, and later growing tubers, quinoa, peanuts, and beans.

Agriculture did not replace hunting (or fishing) and gathering as a source of nutrition, but rather supplemented it. Analyses of skeletons at Paloma have provided evidence that here too men and women worked at different and complementary subsistence tasks. Only men fished in early Paloma coastal societies, but later both men and women fished and performed agricultural tasks. As time went on, differences in the skeletons of men and women lessened, which suggests that gender variations in diet and labor practices became less pronounced.[17]

Several hundred miles up the Peruvian coast from Paloma, there is a complex known as Norte Chico dating from the third millennium BCE, composed of a number of inland sites as well as coastal sites. Substantial evidence suggests that the coastal areas and the inland areas engaged in extensive trade. At Caral, which is twenty-three kilometers upriver from the coast, large numbers of anchovy skeletons and mollusk shells have been discovered. Fishnets made of cotton, produced inland at Caral, have been found in the coastal settlements. In addition to cotton, farmers at Caral produced squash, beans, and guava. There is massive monumental architecture, including a pyramid with a base the size of four and a half football fields, as well as a number of smaller pyramids and two circular plazas. Homes are arranged in eight clusters; each cluster consists of some modest dwellings and some that are more elaborate, suggesting a degree of social differentiation.

The pyramids were used for ceremonial functions; the plazas were public space.[18] Thus a child at Caral would have noted her own home and the way it differed from homes in the cluster, as well as noting the spectacular ceremonial and public spaces. The monumental architecture, along with irrigation and evidence of regular trade between the coastal settlements and Caral, suggest the existence of large-scale undertakings, which some archaeologists find consistent with the existence of a centralized political authority. Here, in contrast with Yangshao and Çatalhöyük, we find features of specialized political functions. But there is no evidence (such as charred buildings or mutilated human bodies) of the warfare or other systematic violence that has conventionally been associated with early state building.

These three examples indicate the diversity of models of the development of complex societies in early human history; the role of domestic spaces and kinship-based groups is apparent in each. They exemplify the vast archaeological evidence about transitions to human settlement and increasing social complexity that occurred independently throughout the world after the end of the last Ice Age. Specific instances followed different ecologies, depending on such local phenomena as the relationship between populations and food sources, but all relied on some combination of hunting or fishing, foraging, and the domestication of animals and plants. Each case exhibited a gender division of labor in which women's contributions were always crucial, not just in reproduction but also in production. In each case, organized domestic life was the basis of new expressions of human organization and novel developments in human culture.

CHAPTER 2

The Birth of the Gods:
Family in the Emergence of Religions (to 1000 CE)

Family life has long provided the metaphors for grappling with questions of cosmological significance: How did the world begin? What accounts for seasonal and life-cyclical reproduction? What happens to people after death? Family stories are also at the core of organized religions from their earliest appearance and persist in religious and spiritual traditions throughout the world. Religions have also long provided the impulse for law codes and prescriptions about family morality. In all of these ways, family history is intimately connected with the emergence and development of religion.

One of the distinguishing characteristics of *Homo sapiens* is the capacity for symbolic and abstract thought. The earliest known symbolic objects—ochre beads carved with geometric designs discovered in caves in southern Africa—date from about 80,000 years ago, not long (by archaeological standards at least) after the emergence of the modern human species around 200,000 years ago.[1] Until recently, archaeologists believed that the world's oldest ritual objects—that is, objects that could be linked to beliefs about the spiritual world or the afterlife—were those found in caves in Southern Europe dating from around 40,000 years ago. However, a snake figure estimated to be 70,000 years old, discovered in 2006 in a cave in Botswana in a region that the contemporary inhabitants, the San, call the "Mountains of the Gods," caused a rethinking of this timetable. Local origin stories in this region include one that traces the descent of mankind from the python and describes how the python carved local hills and streams in its search for water.[2] This discovery suggests that human religious or ritual practices are nearly as old as the human species.

Before the era of the earliest written documents around 6,000 years ago, it is difficult to learn much about the specific contents of religious beliefs. However, some forms of evidence do exist for earlier societies: images and carvings and burial sites offer important clues about how people regarded their ancestors and about how they conceptualized the afterlife. Çatalhöyük in Turkey is a case in point. As at the much earlier Botswana site, carved and painted animals figure importantly in the buildings excavated at Çatalhöyük, suggesting their ritual significance. One interesting aspect of this site is that ritual objects and graves are found in specific areas within domestic spaces. For example, archaeologists found a burial site that contained a male skull over which plaster features had been sculpted and painted. The skull had been reburied in the grave of a woman who died at a later time than the man. It is likely that the skull belonged to a revered ancestor of the woman and her household; in any event it is evidence of ties across generations and an interest in symbolically bridging the gap between the living and the dead. Domestic artworks found at Çatalhöyük tend not to depict scenes of everyday life such as farming. Rather, they are limited to animals or objects apparently having spiritual or ritual significance. In the absence of textual evidence, the specific nature of the beliefs about the afterlife is elusive, but connections between rituals and ancestor veneration seem very likely.

Even when they are located outside of domestic spaces, burial sites are of interest in terms of what they reveal about family relations and the afterlife. More commonly than not, prehistoric burial sites include grave objects in addition to the remains of the deceased. These might include tools such as weapons or amulets and articles of clothing or adornment from which archaeologists have been able to speculate about notions of the afterlife or about possible relationships between dead ancestors and their living descendents.[3] A well-known example of such ancient tombs is the Egyptian royal pyramids, the earliest of which dates from around 3000 BCE. King Aba, for whom the first truly elaborate royal grave was built, was buried not only with tools and other objects of family life but also with living servants and soldiers, presumably to carry on domestic and state activities in the next world, a royal burial practice that was replicated in other ancient cultures, including Mesopotamia, China, West Africa, and Mexico.[4]

Most people had simpler graves, but these also can provide indirect hints about the everyday life of the living as well as their beliefs about the afterlife. In burial sites of more ordinary people who lived in Europe in the first millennium BCE, weapons are often found in graves, especially the graves of adult men. Daggers, swords, and spears might end up in a man's grave within a year or two of their manufacture, suggesting that the owner died while still a young adult who had no heirs. But these weapons could also be buried several generations after their manufacture, presumably because weapons were valuable objects passed down through generations, usually from older to younger men. Some personal ornaments typically found in women's graves (such as bronze armbands) also seem to have been passed down through the female line rather than being buried with the original owner. These burial practices tell us something about the objects used and prized by ancient cultures and about ideas of the afterlife—for example, that the dead might require a certain object. They also can reveal patterns of cross-generational relationships and inheritance practices.[5]

Many origin stories, such as that of ancient Egypt, also root the beginnings of organized religion in family. In the Egyptian story, the sun god Re and the goddess of the night Nut had five children: Osiris, Horus, Seth, Isis, and Nephthys. Osiris married his sister Isis and Seth married his sister Nephthys. According to this mythic model, it was necessary for a god to marry a goddess, which limited the choice to siblings in the case of the original family. However, this origin story established a divine sanction for the custom of sibling marriage that would frequently be followed in families of the Egyptian rulers—the pharaohs—who claimed descent from the gods.

Osiris, so the story goes, went on to become sole ruler of Egypt. However, he found the Egyptian people to be "savage and brutish, fighting among themselves and killing and eating one another." The goddess Isis intervened in this primordial chaos and "discovered the grain of both wheat and barley . . . and Osiris taught people how to plant the seeds when the Nile had risen in the yearly inundation and sunk again leaving fresh fertile mud over the fields . . . He showed them also how to plant vines and make the grapes into wine; and they knew already how to brew beer out of the barley."[6] In other words, divine intervention led humans to the use of agriculture and to an understanding of nature.

Subsequent pharaohs were understood to be divine, descendants of the god Osiris and his wife Isis. According to the ancient stories, Isis found a way for Osiris to father their son, the god Horus, even after Osiris had been killed by his jealous brother Seth. Isis protected Horus and defended his succession before the tribunal of the gods. Isis's place of honor in many temples dedicated to gods and goddesses shows her popularity.

The cult of Isis later spread throughout the Roman Empire, as far away as Britain, and Isis became one of the empire's most popular deities, as suggested by evidence in temples and texts. For example, Apuleius, a Roman writer of the second century CE, wrote in the voice of the goddess: "I am nature, the universal Mother . . . Though I am worshipped in many aspects, known by countless names, and propitiated with all manner of different rites, yet the whole round earth venerates me."[7] The Mother Goddess had been popular in Europe for millennia; Isis was a novel and influential addition to the pantheon.

Family relationships prevail in origin stories in many parts of the world. Maya myths about the creation of the human race show family metaphors in conjunction with other metaphors. Maya creation myths are recorded in the *Popol Vuh*, a manuscript written down in the sixteenth century but containing stories that are much older. The primary gods are a couple, a man and a woman, referred to as He Who Engenders Children and She Who Bears Children. They give birth to twins who are eventually lured into the underworld to play a cosmic ball game, only to be defeated and killed by its evil overlords. However, the head of Hun Hunahpu, one of the twins, is thrown into a calabash tree by the lords of the underworld and immediately causes the tree to bear fruit. A young woman called the Blood Maiden walks by the tree, speaks to its fruit, and becomes pregnant by it. After escaping her father's rage, caused by her unorthodox preg-nancy, she finds her way to the home of her mother-in-law, She Who Bears Children. There Blood Maiden gives birth to a second pair of twins, who avoid the mistakes made by their father and uncle and are able to defeat the lords of the underworld, setting the stage for the fashioning of the first human beings out of maize.[8]

The Judeo-Christian Bible's account of the creation of the world is of interest in terms of both religious and family history. The very first words of the Book of Genesis introduce a novel kind of deity, one who exists and acts alone: "In the beginning God created the heaven and the earth. And the earth was without form, and void; and darkness was upon the face of the deep. And the Spirit of God moved upon the face of the waters."[9] The creation story in Genesis, in addition to play-ing a key role in the emergence of monotheism, is more masculine than most other cosmologies. The Old Testament God does not share or dispute power with other gods or goddesses. The process of creation does not resemble reproduction in human families or in animals or plants.[10] Not only is the creator masculine, according to Genesis, but woman is initially born of man:

In this bronze statue, the Egyptian goddess Isis suckles the infant Horus. Isis served as an important symbolic connection between family relations and the cosmic order in ancient Egypt. Some scholars see Isis and Horus images as predecessors of the Madonna and Christ child images of later Christianity.
Réunion des Musées Nationaux /Art Resource, NY

And the LORD God formed man of the dust of the ground, and breathed into his nostrils the breath of life; and man became a living soul . . . And the LORD God caused a deep sleep to fall upon Adam and he slept: and he took one of his ribs, and closed up the flesh instead thereof; and the rib, which the LORD God had taken from man, made he a woman, and brought her unto the man. And Adam said . . . she shall be called Woman, because she was taken out of Man.[11]

The first woman, Eve, was subservient to the first man from the start; moreover, it was Eve and not Adam whom the Old Testament held responsible for introducing evil into the world, rooting the "fall from grace" in what was portrayed as woman's natural curiosity and susceptibility to seduction.

Feminist historians have pointed to the relationship between the emergence of monotheism in the ancient Middle East and "the creation of patriarchy"—that is, the elevation of the father to a place of power and authority in the family and other social and political institutions. This argument rests on religious texts—especially the Old Testament—that emerged from a specific historical milieu. The books of the Old Testament were written versions of oral traditions handed down from around the second millennium BCE.

The Judaic tribes who wrote the books were making a transition from seminomadic tribal clan society to agricultural settlements governed by kings. The predominant family form bore strong marks of patriliny, or emphasis on the male line of descent. For example, all Israelite women were expected to marry and pass from the control of their father and his lineage to that of their husband. To keep women and their children within their husband's line, it was considered appropriate for men to marry their brothers' widows. Men were allowed multiple wives and concubines, whereas women could have only one husband.

In these respects, the Israelites were similar to other near Eastern cultures of the time, but the religion of Judaism reinforced these patrilineal aspects of kinship by centering people's hopes of salvation upon the promises of a deity who was imagined as a kind of superfather. Moreover, they understood Yahweh's special promise to the Israelites as a covenant among men that passed down through the generations by way of a ritual cut on the male body—circumcision. This particular version of monotheism, which influenced not only ancient Judaism but also early Christianity and Islam, thus brought together theological and kin elements, such as the elevation of a single father god and the suppression of female deities, with family-historical trends like the encouragement of a patriarchal order on earth.

Spiritual beliefs have also provided the inspiration for prescriptions to guide family life. To choose one especially important arena of focus, religious prescriptions have played an important role in the historical development of various understandings of and customs around marriage. It is very likely that rules about marriage have drawn upon beliefs about the place of humans in creation and the cosmos for as long as humans have tried to make sense of the world in such terms.

Ample recorded anthropological evidence from cultures such as the Aranda of Australia shows that people can follow immensely complex rules about marriage without needing written records to keep track of them or state authorities to enforce them. Many Australian tribes evolved marriage rules around totem groups—that is, groups held to be related to or descended from a particular animal or plant (the group's totem). Such group affiliations were part of a larger symbolic system describing relationships between human families and the spiritual world.

In any locality, a totem group would in effect be an extended family clan. A simple example of a clan-based marriage rule is that an emu man could not marry an emu woman. (An emu is a large bird adopted by some Australian clans as their totem.) The Aranda's marriage rules were more complex. In addition to totem groups, they divided the tribe into moieties, or halves, and then each moiety into subsections, and, in some cases, also subsubsections. This complicated the marriage rules even further. An Aranda emu totem group member could marry another emu, but only if the marriage involved an emu from outside of their own moiety (which was inherited from their father). Aranda people of modern times told anthropologists that the rules governing marriage and the assignment of children to moieties were derived from both cosmological and historical events (in particular, negotiations among tribal elders).[12] Even without sacred texts, then, family rules could be governed by complex spiritual systems of thought and rules.

Among religions based on sacred texts, evolving prescriptions and practices of marriage incorporate theological imperatives as well as historical contingencies. Classical Hinduism provides one early example. Early Hindu texts, which date from the second millennium BCE, describe social divisions along family hereditary lines, which later came to be called caste, although caste rules and prescriptions for behavior only became really important later on, around 600 CE.[13]

Caste rules determined ideal marriage partners, and social interactions were also determined to a certain extent by membership in caste. Although caste organization is not an essential part of Hinduism everywhere (the Hinduized societies of Southeast Asia, for example, did not adopt caste structure), the overlay of Hinduism and the caste system, and the rootedness of both in family relationships, made the system quite durable in India.

The *Laws of Manu*, probably composed in the first century CE, are the most important prescriptive text of Hinduism, and they closely link rules about behavior and marriage to cosmology. According to this sacred text:

> The great sages approached Manu when he was seated in single-minded concentration; they exchanged mutual salutations in the proper manner and then they said this to him: "Sir, please tell us, properly and in order, the duties of all four classes and also of the people who are born between (two classes)."[14]

Marriages should unite members of the same caste; Manu goes on at some length about the evil consequences of violating this principle.

In other family systems, rules about whom one can or cannot marry are based largely on kinship relations: a person is prohibited from marrying someone in a particular kin relationship such as sibling or cousin, but the rules in Manu prohibit intermarriages across specific castes. While most societies practice marriage customs leading to marriages between partners of similar social status, Manu argues for marriages within castes in terms of the need to preserve caste purity.

Manu also provided rules about how to behave after marriage. The text makes it very clear that mutual fidelity was the highest goal for marriage, but other prescriptions were quite inegalitarian:

> A virtuous wife should constantly serve her husband like a god, even if he behaves badly, freely indulges his lust, and is devoid of any good qualities ... It is because a wife obeys her husband that she is exalted in heaven ... A woman who is unfaithful to her husband is the object of reproach in this world; (then) she is reborn in the womb of a jackal and is tormented by the diseases born of her evil. The woman who is not unfaithful to her husband and who restrains her mind, speech, and body reaches her husband's worlds (after death) and good people call her a virtuous woman.[15]

In the *Laws of Manu*, marriage is thus seen as similar to a religious relationship: a woman treats her husband as if he is a god, and her reward for "restraining her mind, speech, and body" is to reside with her husband in heaven (a Hindu heaven would not be a permanent abode but a temporary break from the cycle of birth and rebirth). Proper marriage is critical to human social order and holds cosmological significance.

Another example of the close relationship between religious beliefs and rules of family conduct is the Islamic marriage rules that emerged during the three centuries following the death of the Prophet Muhammad in 632 CE. The Islamic legal scholars who codified these rules were influenced by the patriarchal societies in which they lived; thus the texts they compiled emphasized the power of fathers and husbands, even if the Qur'an itself was more egalitarian.[16]

The Qur'an, the record of the revelations of Muhammad, contains many passages that treat women as the religious equivalents of men. For example, one passage in the Qur'an calls on men and women believers in a symmetric fashion:

> For men and women who
> Guard their chastity, and
> For men and women who
> Engage much in God's praise,—
> For them has God prepared
> Forgiveness and a great reward.[17]

Muhammad's first wife, Khadija, was an older widow who was one of his most important early disciples. Several of his later wives, most notably Aisha, played important roles in early Islam and made significant contributions to the hadith—the records of oral accounts of Muhammad's life and his teachings that provide models for Muslim conduct and sources of law. These examples suggest a greater egalitarianism between men and women in early Islam than would be apparent in later years.

For all of the power of his wives, however, aspects of Muhammad's family life have offered models for those of his followers who wished to assert male authority over women in marriage and more generally. The Qur'an allows a man to have four wives and additional concubines if he can support them and treat them equitably. Muhammad had many more wives than four; although nearly all of them were widows at the time of their marriage to the Prophet, he did purportedly consummate his marriage with his third wife Aisha, with her father's encouragement, when she was a young girl just nine or ten years old.[18] The precedent has been controversial. Although some followers argued that the Prophet's marriages were the result of particular circumstances of his life and not to be taken as a model, Islamic legal traditions did use these precedents to justify the taking of multiple, and sometimes very young, wives by ordinary men as well. Similarly, with respect to seclusion, Muhammad late in his life did generally prefer a life of seclusion for his own wives, a custom not practiced by other Muslims at the time. Nevertheless, this was also later used as grounds for generalizing the prescription that married women be veiled and secluded.

As Islam expanded from the Prophet's homeland in the Arabian Peninsula, it moved from a region where woman exercised a great deal of autonomy and where many tribes followed matrilineal principles (that is, wives remained with their families of origin and their children remained in the mother's tribe) to areas such as the Persian Empire and North Africa, where more strongly patrilineal customs and misogynist attitudes prevailed.

The patriarchal practices inherited from the Judaic, Greco-Roman, and Persian cultural legacies in this region influenced the development of Islam much as they left their stamp on early Christianity. The Zoroastrian religious and family practices of the dominant elite classes of the Iraq-Iran region prior to its conquest by Islam seem to have played a particular role. Zoroastrian marriage prized a wife's production of male heirs for her husband's line above all else and emphasized her subservience to her husband, even requiring her obedience if he demanded that she serve as a concubine for another male relative. Her children belonged to her husband. These local practices influenced judges and scholars as they codified Islamic law in the various regions to which the religion spread.

Dramatic changes occurred in Islamic marriage between the time of Muhammad's life and the time when the codification of the sacred writings was completed in the tenth or eleventh century. For example, in Muhammad's time widows often remarried and negotiated the terms of their own remarriage. Beyond the Prophet's own first wife, there are examples like Atika bint Zaid, who married four times, inherited wealth from her first husband, and was able to insist as a condition for marrying her third husband that "he not beat her or prevent her from attending prayers at the mosque."[19] In contrast, in the Islamic Middle East of the eighth or ninth century it was considered shameful for a man to marry a woman who was not a virgin. Moreover, after about the eighth century, there is no longer any evidence of elite women engaging in negotiations for their own marriages and attaching conditions to those marriages.

The conquest itself brought new conditions of family life and family formation. Islamic soldiers merged Arabic and local customs when capturing slaves and taking wives and concubines. Women, even elite women, had less authority to negotiate the terms of their marriages. Zubaida, a

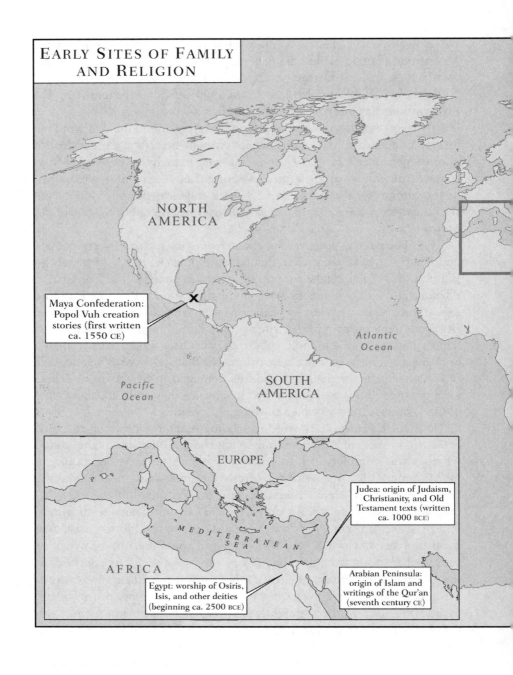

EARLY SITES OF FAMILY
AND RELIGION

NORTH
AMERICA

Maya Confederation:
Popol Vuh creation
stories (first written
ca. 1550 CE)

Atlantic
Ocean

Pacific
Ocean

SOUTH
AMERICA

EUROPE

Judea: origin of Judaism,
Christianity, and Old
Testament texts (written
ca. 1000 BCE)

MEDITERRANEAN
SEA

AFRICA

Egypt: worship of Osiris,
Isis, and other deities
(beginning ca. 2500 BCE)

Arabian Peninsula:
origin of Islam and
writings of the Qur'an
(seventh century CE)

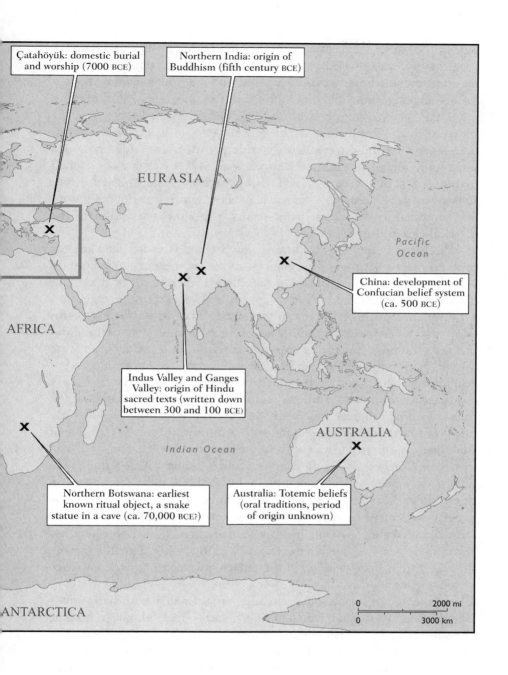

Çatahöyük: domestic burial and worship (7000 BCE)

Northern India: origin of Buddhism (fifth century BCE)

EURASIA

Pacific Ocean

China: development of Confucian belief system (ca. 500 BCE)

AFRICA

Indus Valley and Ganges Valley: origin of Hindu sacred texts (written down between 300 and 100 BCE)

AUSTRALIA

Indian Ocean

Northern Botswana: earliest known ritual object, a snake statue in a cave (ca. 70,000 BCE?)

Australia: Totemic beliefs (oral traditions, period of origin unknown)

ANTARCTICA

0   2000 mi

0   3000 km

wife of the late-eighth-century caliph (ruler) Harun al-Rashid, herself of royal family, was advised to stop nagging when she complained about his attachment to a particular concubine, and indeed, by way of apology for her nagging, presented him with ten more concubines.[20] But in other domestic contexts, lines between wives, concubines, and slaves became blurred. In the conditions of the urban Middle East, where prejudices against women were already widespread, Islam added religious sanction to already inegalitarian social systems.[21] It was laws developed in this context that were codified by Islamic scholars and passed down to subsequent generations as official Islamic law, which was only occasionally contested by dissidents such as Sufis, a group that emphasized the mystical elements of Islam.

While many religious traditions saw the family as an ideal site for religious practice, within other religious traditions, religion and the family were sites of competition or antagonism rather than mutual reinforcement. The ideal Hindu life course prescribed a set of life stages that a Brahman, a member of the highest caste, was to go through: student, married householder, and wandering ascetic. A devout Hindu did not leave home to pursue intensive meditation until his children were grown. Within the course of a lifetime, obligations to family life and to religious practice could both be met, but not at the same time.

In other religious traditions, conflict between the demands of the family and of religion was even sharper. Buddhism is one of those traditions, although it too begins with a family story. The founder of Buddhism, Siddhartha, was born in the fifth century BCE and lived as a prince in Northern India in luxurious surroundings. According to the philosopher-poet Aśvaghoṣa's biography of the Buddha (composed in the first century CE) the infant Buddha is born "from the side of the queen consecrated by rites,/ without pain and without ill,/ for the welfare of the world."[22] At his birth, a seer predicts that he would either leave home and become an ascetic or be a great king. For this reason, his father kept him secluded in the palace, away from any knowledge of the outside world.

At the age of twenty-nine, already married and with a baby son—whom he named Rahula, which means "fetter"—he left home to become an ascetic. His wife Yashodhara lamented his leaving, saying "If it's not my lot to see my lord's face/ his sweetly smiling face with those long eyes, / Still this poor Rahula does not deserve / never to be rocked in his father's lap!"[23] His father the king lamented that he was "burned up with the fire of grief" that his son had left home.[24] The Buddha acknowledged this grief when he said "I recognize the love fathers have for their sons, / above all the love the king bears for me; / Although I know it, I am forced to forsake my kin, by the fear of sickness, old age and death."[25]

In some accounts of the Buddha's life, when Rahula was seven, Siddhartha returned. Rahula asked for his inheritance, and Siddhartha, saying that earthly inheritance was fraught with troubles, offered him enlightenment instead. Rahula left the family and became the first novice monk. Siddhartha's father was so unhappy at this second loss that he made Siddhartha promise that in the future, monks would not be allowed to leave home without the permission of their parents. This suggests both the importance of renunciation of family to Buddhist attainment and the tensions that surround it.

After several years of intense asceticism, that is to say meditation accompanied by the renunciation of physical comfort, the Buddha had an enlightenment experience, which brought him insight into suffering and the means with which to eliminate it. The insights suggested that, while life is characterized by suffering, suffering can be eliminated by eliminating the desires that lead to it. The discipline of Buddhist practice provides guidance into eliminating earthly desires. The Buddha left his family to attain enlightenment, and the highest goal of Buddhist practice also mandated a celibate monastic life, making a commitment to a life without children.

As Buddhism spread to China in the third century CE, it came into conflict with Chinese ideas about family life. Buddhist ideals that suggested that the highest calling for a person was to lead a celibate life in a monastery struck most Chinese as extraordinarily anti-family. If one had no offspring, then one was cutting off not only one's own line of descent, but also that of one's ancestors. The Buddhist response to charges that Buddhism was incompatible with Chinese family values was to assert that if one attained enlightenment, the benefits would accrue to one's relatives.

One of the key stories coming out of the history of the Chinese adaptation of Buddhism is the story of Mulian (whose original Indian name was Maudgalyayana), dating from around the fourth century CE. Mulian was a Buddhist monk who went to hell to rescue his mother who had been sent there because she had squandered on parties and banquets the food and money that she should have given to monks. He rescues her, and the story of his horrendous filial journey through hell was told and retold through religious tracts, and, in later times, fiction and drama.[26] The popularity of the Mulian story in China reflects how important it was to Chinese Buddhists to find a way to reconcile the competing demands of religion and family.

Christianity, like Judaism and Islam, traces its origins as an organized religion to the ancient Middle East. It was built upon Judaic foundations and scriptures that brought with them patriarchal tendencies; moreover, by the time of Christ, Greek and Roman imperial presence in the region had also brought legal and philosophical support for belief in male superiority. Early converts to Christianity grappled with these legacies as they interpreted Christ's message, which built on these legacies in some respects but departed from them in others.

In his life of preaching, as recorded in the Gospels, Christ preached to men and women, rich and poor. This sentiment is echoed in St. Paul's epistle to the Galatians, which discussed an open approach to welcoming converts: "There is neither Jew nor Greek, there is neither bond nor free, there is neither male nor female, for you are all one in Christ Jesus."[27] Although Christ was God's son, he had been born of a human woman and grew up with a human family; some of his most important followers were women.

In a striking departure from local precedent, he also taught that faith came before earthly ties, including family. For example, Luke's Gospel quotes Christ as having said, "If any man come to me, and hate not his father, and mother, and wife, and children, and brethren, and sisters, yea, and his own life also, he cannot be my disciple." He promised his disciples a reward for their renunciation of family: "Verily I say unto you," Jesus said to them, "There is no man that hath left house, or parents, or brethren, or wife, or children, for the kingdom of God's sake/ Who shall not receive manifold more in this present time, and in the world to come life everlasting."[28]

Although such passages are open to a variety of interpretations, some early Church leaders read them to mean that a celibate life of devotion to Christianity and away from all family ties was the best form of Christian life. Some traditions of early Christian commentary reveal a strong strain of hostility toward the female body, sexuality, and family life, despite the recognition of their necessity. Augustine, a Christian philosopher and theologian who lived from the fourth to the fifth century CE, for example, wrote "I fail to see what use woman can be to man . . . if one excludes the function of bearing children."[29] In his writings on marriage Augustine held up celibacy as the highest spiritual state: "For intercourse of marriage for the sake of begetting hath not fault; but for the satisfying of lust, but yet with husband or wife, by reason of the faith of the bed, it hath venial fault: but adultery or fornication hath deadly fault, and, through this, continence from all intercourse is indeed better even than the intercourse of marriage itself, which takes place for the sake of begetting."[30]

In the hands of an unabashedly misogynist writer such as Tertullian, who lived from the second to the third century CE even the redeeming virtues of reproduction were not enough to justify marital sexuality. Tertullian's views on sexuality drew upon the tradition of blaming Eve for the introduction of sin into the world. "You," Tertullian wrote to Christian women, "destroyed so easily God's image, man." According to Tertullian only human law makes the distinction between marital sex and fornication; he believed that "the best thing for a man is not to touch a woman; and accordingly the virgin's is the principal sanctity, because it is free from affinity with fornication."[31]

Despite this hostility to sexuality, often associated with misogyny, early Christian teaching could also empower women by providing then with an alternative to a subservient marriage—a vow of chastity. The importance of this novel option is apparent in the stories of women martyrs. It comes across especially forcefully in regions that had been dominated by Zoroastrianism, where virtually all women martyrs whose lives are recorded had angered authorities and families by taking vows of chastity.[32] The threat of female conversion to Christianity was especially subversive to Zoroastrians in that it encouraged women both to defy male religious authorities, the Zoroastrian priests, and to defy their most essential duty under the Zoroastrian family order—to reproduce.

The defiant attitude of the women martyrs is noteworthy. One of them, a woman named Tarbo who lived during the fourth century CE in what is now Iraq, received an offer of marriage from the Zoroastrian priest who examined her regarding her heretical beliefs. He told her that he would save her life if she agreed to become his wife. Her response as recorded is her biography is scornful: "Shut your mouth, you wicked man and enemy of God; don't ever again utter anything so disgusting . . . I am the betrothed of Christ. In his name I am preserving my virginity . . . I die a heroic death, for thus shall I obtain true life."[33]

While most early religious traditions focused on the family as an important site of religious symbolism and practice, some religious traditions emerged in tension or in competition with the family. That tension does not diminish the importance of the family to religious history, but rather underscores it.

CHAPTER 3

Ruling Families:
Kinship at the Dawn of Politics
(ca. 3000 BCE to 1450 CE)

An ancient clay tablet from Sumer in the Euphrates Valley dating from the early second millennium BCE records a list of dynasties and kings; it is one of the earliest existing documents of the close connections between family lineage and royal power. The first king on this list whose existence can be further documented ruled around 2600 BCE, but the list begins much earlier in time, with the mythological descent of kingship from heaven to the first earthly king, Alulim. The Sumerian king list notes dynastic breaks and the move of rule from one capital city to another, but most frequently it tells of royal successions that pass from father to son: Gilgamesh, whose father was the lord of Kuluba, is recorded as having ruled for 126 years; he was succeeded by his son Ur-nungal, who ruled for thirty years and then was succeeded by his son Udul-kalama. Preserved across millennia, the king list carved in clay legitimated royal authority through a genealogy that functioned simultaneously as political and family history.

Such records point to the family character of the early states that evolved in ancient Mesopotamia. Agricultural settlements in this region just east of the Mediterranean began to grow in size and density around 5,000 years ago. The world's first large cities emerged here, cities whose populations numbering in the hundreds of thousands dwarfed earlier agrarian centers like Çatalhöyük. Many activities that had previously been the province of families or small groups of households came under the control of political rulers and their officials—the first ancient states—or of religious authorities. Still, Mesopotamian rulers based their power on alliances built through kin relations. Family models and family relationships played key roles in the emergence of these new city-states.

Ancient Mesopotamian kings also installed family members as priests or priestesses at important shrines and as governors of military outposts. The Akkadian dynasty's founder, King Sargon, appointed his daughter Enkheduanna as a priestess of several religiously important and politically strategic temples—one dedicated to the Moon God in the city of Ur and another dedicated to An, the Supreme God of Heaven, at Uruk. Enkheduanna worshipped the Sumerian goddess Inanna as well as the Akkadian goddess Ishtar. Because (unlike her father) she spoke both Sumerian and Akkadian, Enkheduanna played a key role as religious and cultural intermediary between the two divisions of her father's empire. Enkheduanna was not unique—she was the first of many generations of daughters in this dynasty to serve as priestesses of the kingdoms of early Mesopotamia. Family relations were in this way critical to early state-building ventures. Male leaders of royal dynastic families generally called the shots, but their daughters or wives were not mere pawns; they were also frequently influential, powerful, and politically active.[1]

The royal families of Mesopotamia were hardly typical of other families at the time. Enkheduanna was a princess and a priestess; her father was a king. In the Mesopotamian cities where she lived, she and her royal family and household depended on the labor of families of traders, scribes, craftsmen, soldiers, day laborers, and musicians. Their food came from farm families in the surrounding countryside. Social and economic differentiation accompanied the evolution of urban societies, which meant greater inequalities in terms of both generational and gender relations within families and social class differences among families. Squads of laborers paid in food rations worked under the supervision of officials in the employ of kings or priests to build the irrigation systems upon which the cities depended and the impressive monuments like the twenty-first-century BCE Ziggurat of Ur, sections of which have survived into the present. From the point of view of laboring-class families, the emergence of urban communities did not necessarily translate into an easier life, just as the transition to agriculture did not necessarily imply a higher standard of living for everyone.[2]

Rulers of ancient Mesopotamia eventually introduced laws that brought aspects of family life under state authority and, despite the fact that royal wives and daughters had previously played important roles, gradually altered the balance of power between men and women to the disadvantage of women. Family relations were still critical in politics, but the models were changing. The earliest known written law codes that we have—from Mesopotamia in the second millennium

BCE—gave men, especially fathers, very significant amounts of power over wives and children.

The Code of Hammurabi, dating from around 1750 BCE, included a number of provisions about families. These laws regulated property ownership and its transmission within families. Children of both sexes had rights to family property, but different sorts of rights. Sons inherited the bulk of their father's wealth and property at the time of the father's death; daughters got their share of the family's wealth in the form of a dowry when they married. Even though a daughter's share in inheritance was not the same as that of her brothers, she did maintain some control over her dowry wealth after marriage, and some assurance that she could use it as a form of economic security in her lifetime even if it eventually passed back to her husband or sons at her death. The Code also presumed that families would supervise their daughters strictly to ensure premarital chastity and that fathers had the ultimate say in the selection of their children's spouses. These laws simultaneously increased the power of fathers over family members and family wealth and cemented the social position of elite families by keeping more property under tight family control.[3]

These characteristics of Mesopotamian family law are quite significant for long-term historical development. Many subsequent societies in this region developed laws and family relations resembling those of Mesopotamia. Family arrangements similar to those introduced in ancient Mesopotamian law came to seem "natural" in ancient societies such as Greece and Rome. Fathers' authority over children, and husbands' over wives, was not merely a family affair—it was backed by the power of law. State authority and family law thus evolved together.

The case of Mesopotamia is typical of ancient civilizations in that political authority and its transmission through time took family relationships for granted as the appropriate channels of and models for the exercise of political power. Mesopotamia is one of the earliest state-organized societies to be documented in the historical record. But in the period between the third millennium BCE and the second millennium CE, a whole variety of others emerged over the globe. Whatever form these states took—kingdoms, empires, confederations, or republics—state builders nearly always established a relationship between their own family and rulership, or at least thought about how to rule a state through family models and analogies.

Ancient states most frequently centered on monarchial dynasties—that is, rule was in the hands of a single authority figure like a king, who typically had inherited the right to rule and in turn passed it on to a son or daughter or other relative. Connecting political authority with family no doubt made it seem more natural and legitimate; family authority and kingly authority could thus reinforce each other. Beyond kingship, other instruments of state power also relied on family connections or models. For many ancient state builders, military conquest was an important component of the political order and social fabric. States exerted control over their territory at least in part by their control over forms of coercion like armies and police. Rulers built armies to sustain their power at home and to conquer neighbors.

Military organizations drew on and altered family and gender relations. Because military activities were virtually always male undertakings, valuing military prowess over other sorts of skills contributed to gender inequalities. Some mythological traditions of ancient Greece and Scandinavia refer to matriarchal or even all-female societies with female armies; scattered burial evidence points to the actual existence of female warriors in several ancient societies in the Caucasus, Scythia, South Asia, South America, and West Africa. However, the weight of historical evidence would suggest that the building of armies that accompanied the growth of centralized state societies typically enhanced masculine privileges and power. Indeed, in view of the political, legal, and military character of many ancient civilizations, some feminist anthropologists and historians have argued that a reordering of gender relations to the disadvantage of women was an intrinsic component of the emergence of ancient state societies.

But not everywhere to the same extent. Political authority and legal codes treated family and gender relations in ancient Egypt, for example, in a manner that presents some interesting contrasts with developments in Mesopotamia and elsewhere in the ancient world. In fact, when the Greek historian Herodotus visited Egypt in the fifth century BCE he was surprised by the family dynamics he found there and commented in his history that "the Egyptians, in their manner and customs, seem to have reversed the ordinary practices of mankind. For instance, women attend market and are employed in trade, while men stay at home and do the weaving."[4]

When Greek conquerors of Egypt attempted to impose their rule there during the fourth century BCE, the different family and gender orders collided. The women of Egypt at the time moved around freely and without veils, in contrast to respectable women in Greece, who were discouraged from public appearances and were expected to cover their heads when in public.[5] In Greece a woman was always under the protection of a male guardian (usually her father or her husband), who

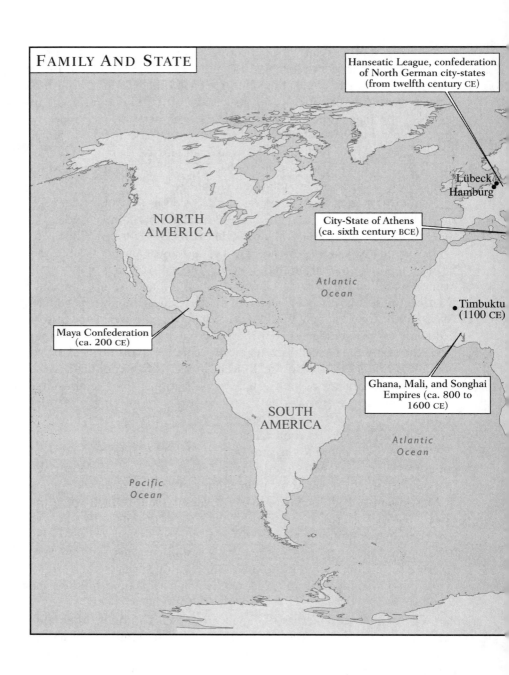

FAMILY AND STATE

Hanseatic League, confederation
of North German city-states
(from twelfth century CE)

Lübeck
Hamburg

City-State of Athens
(ca. sixth century BCE)

NORTH
AMERICA

Atlantic
Ocean

Timbuktu
(1100 CE)

Maya Confederation
(ca. 200 CE)

Ghana, Mali, and Songhai
Empires (ca. 800 to
1600 CE)

SOUTH
AMERICA

Atlantic
Ocean

Pacific
Ocean

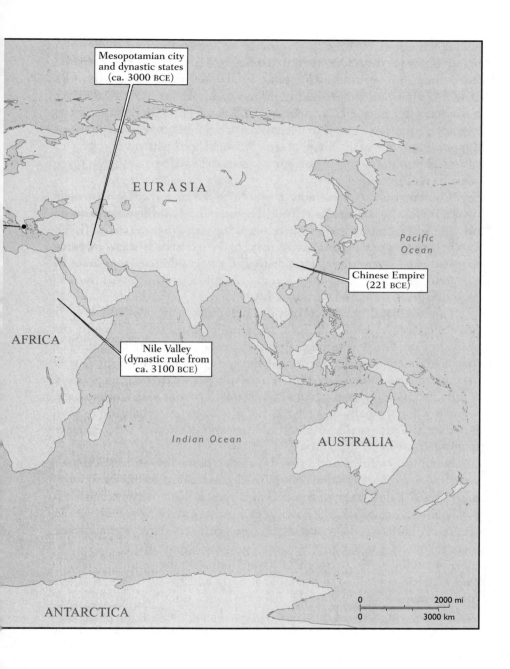

Mesopotamian city
and dynastic states
(ca. 3000 BCE)

EURASIA

Pacific
Ocean

Chinese Empire
(221 BCE)

AFRICA

Nile Valley
(dynastic rule from
ca. 3100 BCE)

Indian Ocean

AUSTRALIA

ANTARCTICA

| 0 | | 2000 mi |
| 0 | | 3000 km |

held much power over her; for example, he had to approve of all of her major financial transactions. But women in Egypt could choose to be ruled under long-prevailing Egyptian legal codes that were much more gender-egalitarian; they could continue to appear in public, transact business, and act on their own behalf in financial and legal matters. For example, a papyrus record of a legal case from 249 BCE recounts how an Egyptian woman named Tay-hetem "loaned her husband 3 *deben* of silver (273 grammes) at 30 percent interest, to be paid back within three years as was usual."[6]

Women could even dispute in public with male members of their own families. In another case from the same era, two Egyptian women brought suit against a male relative who, taking advantage of the Greek law's more favorable treatment of men, had tried to confiscate property that had been left to the women by their father; and in another case, an Egyptian woman sued her own father for similarly trying to deprive her of goods given to her by her husband.[7]

This legal independence of these Egyptian women vis-à-vis their male relatives had been in place for a millennium by the time of the arrival of the Greek conquerors. In fact, records from the beginning of the third millennium BCE show that Egyptian women—married as well as unmarried—could buy and inherit property, manage their own affairs, act as their own agents in lawsuits, and the like. At marriage, women seem normally to have moved in with their husbands' families, but they still retained considerable legal and economic independence from their husband's families.

In terms of political authority, most Egyptian rulers—the pharaohs—were in fact men, but they established their claim to the throne by marrying the daughter of the previous queen. This often resulted in royal sibling or half-sibling marriages, since a crown prince needed to secure his authority by marrying a crown princess. Even though there were relatively few female rulers in pharaonic Egypt (just four listed of more than 500 rulers between 3100 and 343 BCE), the legality of female rule was acknowledged in principle as early as 2900 BCE. Female rulers like Hatshepsut were exceptional, but not incompatible with Egyptian understandings of the relationship between gender and political power.

Hatshepsut was the daughter and wife of a king, and also regent for a young male successor, before she took over as king in 1490 BCE. She ruled as a female king, taking on the usual title and having herself portrayed in the attire—a kilt and false beard—that symbolized royal authority. Interestingly, the false beard was not Hatshepsut's invention as a means of claiming a masculine identity; male pharaohs wore false beards, too. Beards are certainly a masculine symbol, but in ancient Egypt a beard was something that rulers put on rather than grew. Moreover, Hatshepsut never attempted to disguise the fact that she was a woman, claiming in inscriptions, for example, to be a daughter of the god Amun. Her rule and that of the other female monarchs, although exceptional, offer evidence that in ancient Egypt female kingship was not a contradiction in terms.[8]

Even without assuming rule, the mothers, sisters, and daughters of kings and queens could often be quite important in rule and successorship. Queen Nefertiti, among the most celebrated of Egypt's queens, was often portrayed as the twin and equal of her husband King Akhenaten, who ruled from 1352 to 1338 BCE. There is even some speculation that she may have ruled alongside him as coregent toward the end of his reign.

In comparison with the informal power of royal consorts in other systems, the queen's position in Egypt was buttressed by succession rules and by her official status as "Great Royal Wife." The matrilineally transmitted office of "Wife of the God," which gave her authority

Hatshepsut, a female pharaoh who reigned in the late fifteenth century BCE had herself depicted as a sphinx with her head on the body of a lion. The false beard was one of the symbols of ancient Egyptian royal authority; it was worn by both male and female pharaohs. © The Metropolitan Museum of Art /Art Resource, NY

within the male-dominated temple priesthood, also provided a base of power to female members of the royal family during some periods of pharaonic Egypt's history. Women were for the most part not politically powerful apart from their family connections, but their specific and unusual dynastic roles—such as the mother-in-law though whom the pharaonic succession had to pass—underscore the ways in which male political authority in dynastic systems was also contingent on family connections.

In ancient China, the emperorship was transmitted through hereditary principles within a ruling family lineage, or dynasty, but the notion of family and heredity as the basis of political authority was to some degree tempered by notions of merit. The nature of the tension between heredity and merit is exemplified by the mythical sage kings Yao and Shun, the progenitors of political order in China. Because neither of

This engraved house altar from around 1350 BCE depicts the Pharaoh Akhenaten, Queen Nefertiti, and three of their daughters. The symmetry of the image of the king and queen may suggest the symmetry in the relationship between them, possibly as corulers. bpk, Berlin /Aegyptisches Museum, Staatliche Museen /Art Resource, NY

them had a son worthy of inheriting the throne, each of them passed on the throne to someone he selected for his ability, Yao to Shun and Shun to Yu. Yu had an able son to whom he transmitted the throne, thus beginning the idea of the transmission of the throne within a dynasty.

The notion of the mandate of heaven provides a further qualification to the idea of dynastic transmission. A dynasty was considered legitimate as long as it held the mandate of heaven; once it lost the mandate, it lost its legitimacy. Signs from heaven that a ruling family held its mandate included regular rainfall and good crops, thus ensuring a contented population. Droughts, bad harvests, and popular unrest were sure signs that the dynasty had lost its mandate. Throughout Chinese history, rebels have periodically asserted that the ruling dynasty had lost the mandate and that they themselves had inherited it. By this mechanism, new ruling families could be installed even while the principle of dynastic inheritance was preserved. China was unified as an empire in 221 BCE under the Qin dynasty, and for the next 2,000 years the Chinese empire was ruled by a series of dynasties. Even during periods of disunion (such as the one between 220 and 589 CE), smaller states organized themselves along dynastic principles.

Dynastic power in China was normally transmitted from father to son, although occasionally a brother, nephew, or other male relative would inherit the throne. Empresses (in some cases as the wife of the emperor, but more prominently as his mother) could play extremely important roles in government, but their connection to legitimate rule was always through the emperor, who was male. The seventh-century Empress Wu was the only woman to claim the title of "emperor," and her reign has generally been regarded as usurpation. This differs from the role of Egyptian queens, who could legitimately rule in their own right, and who as daughters of queens played an essential role through marriage in legitimizing a new king.

Beyond the long-lasting practice of patrilineal transmission of rule, familial metaphors were important in the conceptualization of rule in China in several other ways: the emperor was the Son of Heaven, and there were rituals that only he could perform. During the Han dynasty (206 BCE to 220 CE), a system of thought known as Confucianism became a state ideology, and families adopted it as a private ethical system as well. The fundamental text of Confucianism is known as the *Analects*; it consists of aphorisms collected by the students of the philosopher Confucius who lived in China in the fifth century BCE. Commentary on the *Analects* and other early Confucian texts formed the core of much of Chinese philosophy until the modern era.

Confucian theory posited that the state was the family writ large, and that a well-governed empire was built on well-governed families. According to Confucian thought, the "Five Relationships" (ruler/subject, father/son, husband/wife, elder brother/younger brother, and friend/friend) were the building blocks of society in both the domestic and the political realm. Political relations were seen as analogous to familial relations (especially the parent/child and husband/wife relations), and discussions of family virtue took on an added urgency because of the political implications.

Filial piety (the duty a child owes its parents) and wifely fidelity became extremely important virtues because of their political importance. A common proverb said "Just as a man should serve only one ruler, a woman should serve only one husband." Texts like the *Biographies of Virtuous Women* (first compiled in the first century CE, but revised and reprinted throughout China's history) recounted stories of widows who went to extraordinary lengths (in extreme cases, committing suicide) to avoid remarriage; these stories were regarded as significant for the lessons they provided to both men and women about the importance of political loyalty.

But the emperor did not rule single-handedly; he was assisted by a bureaucracy that was selected on the basis of merit. (In later Chinese societies, the bureaucracy would be selected on the basis of civil service examinations; this was not yet the case in the Han dynasty.) Provincial governors and magistrates were selected by the central government; officials frequently served in regions of China far from their native places. Magistrates were called "Father and Mother Officials," reinforcing the importance of family authority as a key model of political authority even when the officials in question were not selected according to hereditary models.

The Maya provide a contrasting example of interactions between family and political authority. The classic period Maya (from roughly the first through the tenth centuries CE) were organized in city-states that dotted the region that is now southern Mexico and parts of Honduras, Belize, and Guatemala. Although the Maya region was not one unified political entity, the people we call Maya did share a number of important characteristics, among which were written language, a calendar, and forms of artistic expression. The city-states engaged in trade with one another and occasionally with regions in central Mexico that lay outside the Maya cultural area. Warfare among the various city-states was not an uncommon occurrence, and it intensified toward the end of the classic period. Rulership in these city-states was hereditary; it was normally passed from father to son, though in cases where there was no son, it could be passed on to a younger brother or a daughter.

Maya kinship was largely patrilineal; a woman moved into her husband's household upon marriage and her children would be counted as members of their father's family. However, in contrast with many other patrilineal societies where a woman left her family of birth when she married, a married Maya woman retained lifelong ties with the family of her birth. Moreover, her children had a formalized secondary affiliation with their mother's family of birth, particularly with her brothers, who would be responsible for training their sisters' sons in hunting and martial arts.

Men of the Mayan elite could have more than one wife.[9] Because marriage within the patrilineal kin group was discouraged, marriage networks created a web of important alliances across these groups and even across localities. Members of the ruling elite in one city-state would often form marriage alliances with rulers of other city-states, which created or deepened connections among city states and provided important venues for the integration of Maya culture. Marriages would sometimes be contracted with non-Maya groups in central Mexico with whom the Maya traded.

The rich visual record of the Maya illustrates connections between family and the state. One tablet from the city-state of Palenque portrays an event that took place in 615 CE, when a queen known as Lady Zac Kuk transmitted the throne to her son Pacal. Zac Kuk had inherited the throne in 612 from her father and ruled for three years. Pacal, who was twelve years old at the time of his accession, is shown seated on a double-headed jaguar throne. Zac Kuk's attire suggests that she may be impersonating the Maize God, one of the most important of the Maya divinities. Maya rulers regularly impersonated deities as a way of asserting political legitimacy. Zac Kuk seems to be invoking the authority of the Maize God as well as her own authority as she transmits power to her son. Zac Kuk remained a powerful figure even in the afterlife.[10] It was not uncommon for the rulers of Palenque to be treated as divinities after their death; thus kin connections become connections not only with ancestors but also with deities.

Despite their very real differences, ancient Mesopotamian, Egyptian, Chinese, and Mayan states all were built around some form of hereditary kingship. In each of these cases, connecting political authority with family inheritance made it seem more natural and legitimate. The family models in operation were quite varied. Royal marriages in each case produced the new generation of candidates for the throne,

This Mesoamerican tablet from the seventh century portrays the passing of rulership from mother to son. The lady Zac Kuk, seated on the left of the tablet, hands a drum crown to her son, Pacal. Pacal is seated on a double-headed jaguar throne. The writing on the tablet (horizontal on the top left and vertical on the top right) identify Zac Kuk and Pacal as mother and son. Courtesy of the Peabody Museum of Archaeology and Ethnology, Harvard University, No. 92-50-20/C1110.

but marriage was not the same type of relationship everywhere. For example, Egyptian royal marriages sometimes entailed marriages between siblings or half siblings and legitimacy passed from the former queen to her son-in-law, whereas in China rule normally passed from father to son. In ancient China and among the Maya, royal (and other) marriages might involve more than two partners. Still, for all the variation in detail, family and kinship relationships were explicitly tied to political authority and state-building strategies from the moment when dynastic states first emerged. In none of these cases was family the only grounds of legitimate political authority, but it was a necessary one.

But what of forms of rule other than kingship? Even where power was not justified by inheritance of rule from father to son, family and political authority could still be closely connected. The experimentation with democratic political forms in classical Athens that began in the sixth century BCE certainly represented an exception, significant in world-historical terms, to the more general pattern of association between the emergence of state societies and kingship. Athenian society still relied on links between family and political authority, but those links were of a different sort from those of dynastic monarchies.

One feature of the Athenian family and gender system—the increasing restriction of women in comparison with earlier Greek cultures—was ironically related to building more egalitarian relations among men. Suppressing the inequalities of wealth that had been typical of earlier aristocratic rule meant suppressing lavish displays of wealth and status. Since a woman's dress and ornamentation were a sign of her husband's wealth, the move toward greater equality among men added fuel to the argument that women should not be out in public. Their public appearances were restricted to funerals and some other ritual occasions.[11] Reformed household, gender, and kin relations were thus central features of life in classical Athens. Respectable women were secluded and kept under the authority of male guardians. Men transmitted political rights, property, and ritual obligations to their male descendants. Legitimate male heirs were necessary to perpetuate the cult of the family's patrilineal ancestors and to continue the family's participation in governance in a state constructed on the equal citizenship of adult free men (women and slaves were excluded from citizenship). Only in the absence of male heirs could a daughter fill in, so to speak, by marrying, preferably a man in her father's lineage, and producing a male child who could fulfill cult and civic obligations to both his mother's and his father's patriline.

In this strongly patrilineal culture, there is evidence that even biology was understood in ways that emphasized the power of the father. A child was assumed to be a product of his father's "seed," which the mother, a stranger from another lineage, merely nourished, as is suggested in Aeschylus's play *Eumenides*:

> She who is called the mother is not her offspring's
> Parent, but nurse to the newly sown embryo.
> The male—who mounts—begets. The female, a stranger,
> Guards a stranger's child if no god bring it harm.[12]

Rules governing the inheritance of Athenian citizenship sometimes required both parents to be citizens and sometimes were relaxed so as to allow Athenian men to transmit citizenship to their offspring even if their wives were "foreign." For all of its radical experimentation with forms of rule, Athenian democracy still involved a close connection between family and polity. Access to the right to rule was not limited to one family, as it was for monarchies, but it still normally passed from father to son.

Another ancient society that was not governed by kings is the fabled city of Timbuktu in West Africa. Although Timbuktu was at various points in its history either under the protection of or incorporated into surrounding dynastic empires, it maintained a high degree of political autonomy and distinctive local political institutions. At around the same time that royal families were building dynastic states in Central America, similar developments were occurring in several regions of Africa. In the century following Muhammad's death in 632 CE, much of Northern Africa came under the control of an Islamic ruler called a caliph. The first caliphs were selected by a council of tribal leaders, but in the late seventh century the caliph Mu'awiyya set a new precedent when he convinced the council to designate his son Yazid as his successor. Technically the successor was still elected, but in practice a hereditary dynasty was established. From then on, rulers of the new dynasty, the Umayyad, always designated one of their sons as successor.[13]

In West Africa, the first of a series of dynastic empires to rule this region, the Empire of Ghana, emerged in the eighth century CE, followed by the Mali Empire (thirteenth through sixteenth centuries) and the Songhai Empire (late fourteenth through late sixteenth centuries). These empires followed "bloodline" or family inheritance rules in determining heirs to the throne, even if there were often disputes between competing sons or adopted sons at the point of succession. However, despite being surrounded by dynastic models, a novel relationship between family and the state came onto the scene in this region in Timbuktu.

Timbuktu emerged around 1100 CE near the northern bank of the Niger River, which served as an important trade route to the south, linking the agricultural society of sub-Saharan West Africa with the great desert to the north, peopled with nomadic herders and traders. It soon became an ethnic, linguistic, and intellectual crossroads as well, and the city attracted traders, immigrants, and Muslim scholars from near and far. Timbuktu grew rapidly between the twelfth and fourteenth centuries, attracting an ethnically and racially diverse population of Tuaregs from the north and Fulanis and Songhais from the west and south who came to the city for security, for study, or for trade. It held perhaps 10,000 residents around 1300, and the number continued to grow until the sixteenth century, when the city's population reached between 30,000 and 50,000 people.[14]

Medieval Arabic chronicles claim that Timbuktu was an Islamic outpost from the time of its founding by North African Tuareg tribesmen. By the thirteenth century, the city had developed a tradition of learning to rival older Muslim cities. Its role as a center of Islamic learning connected city inhabitants with the wider Muslim world to the north and east; its role as a trade hub connected them with the Muslim and non-Muslim inhabitants of West Africa.

As a respected Islamic center and a rich source of trade wealth, Timbuktu long enjoyed a high degree of autonomy from the various regional empires (first Mali and then Songhai) with which it was associated and whose rulers were generally more than happy to encourage Timbuktu's scholarly reputation and its commercial activity. They certainly were happy to profit from the city's wealth and to intermarry with local families. Leo Africanus—who traveled the sixteenth-century Mediterranean in various capacities, as a merchant, a diplomat, and a slave—noted in his 1526 description of the city that "the inhabitants are very rich, especially the strangers who have settled in the country; so much so that the current king [the emperor of Songhai] has given two of his daughters in marriage to two brothers, both businessmen, on account of their wealth."[15]

The city developed a distinctive form of local rule. Power was essentially in the hands of an ethnically diverse group of families who held wealth based on trade and whose status as economic elites was buttressed by their involvement in and support of Islamic scholarship. These families established schools and private libraries devoted to the preservation and teaching of Islamic texts. There were around 150 such schools in Timbuktu at the end of the fifteenth century (for comparison, there were only twenty by the time French took over the city in 1893).[16]

The Islamic schools were family affairs where men transmitted Islamic learning across the generations to their own sons and to other boys and young men. Aspiring scholars would normally study mostly under one master, usually a relative, but would also spend time in another scholar's household. A student would live at home if his family was from Timbuktu, but spend the days in the household of his master and often marry into his master's family as well. Immigrant pupils often lived in the master's household. Family relationships were very important in this system of educating the city's future leaders and scholars.

One example is the renowned scholar Ahmed Baba, born in the mid-sixteenth century. He studied under a scholar named Muhammad Baghayughu, who had originally been taught by Ahmed Baba's father Ahmad ibn al-Hajj Ahmad. Ahmad Baba in turn taught his teacher's nephew. This cross-generational exchange of master-pupil relationships, often supplemented by intermarriages and joint commercial ventures among the families, cemented the ties among the elite class and also supported the system of learning.[17] In addition to running schools and mosques, these families built libraries by collecting books and passing them down through the generations. For example, Ahmed Baba inherited 700 volumes from his grandfather and had increased his personal library to 1,600 volumes by the end of his life. His library was lost when he was deported at the time of the Moroccan conquest of Timbuktu in 1594.[18]

The elite families also monopolized local offices, especially the important office of judge (*qadi*). These judges had religious authority (they confirmed the city's religious leaders, the imams) and they also held lawmaking and judicial authority. They resolved religious and secular disputes between merchants or within families. *Qadis* had to have education, to know the law, to possess wealth, and to be beyond corruption, so it seemed only natural to recruit them from among the elite families of scholars and merchants. In effect, most judges inherited their post from a brother, father, or teacher. The majority of the city's judges over the 500-year period beginning in the fifteenth century came from just six families.[19]

One particularly interesting long-term result of this family-based system of governance and learning has been the establishment of family historical continuities of remarkably long duration. Even today, libraries and records of the past are still held in the hands of the descendants of medieval scholars and judges. For example, a local scholar named Ismael Haïdara, who was interviewed by a journalist in 2005, could recount that one of his ancestors was Mahmud Kati, a scholar whose father had moved to Timbuktu after being expelled from Spain in the 1400s and whose mother was the sister of the then Songhai king Askia Mohamed. Mr. Haïdara's ancestors had written notes in the margins of their manuscripts and thus passed down a record of the family's past along with the family library—births and deaths in the imperial family, drafts of imperial letters, and records of trade.[20] In 2007, Haïdara showed a *New York Times* reporter a leather case which held a history of the Spanish and Songhai branches of the family. He told the reporter, "This is our family's story . . . It was written in 1519."[21]

The family life of Timbuktu was certainly distinctive in many respects, but echoes of it can be found among patrician classes in cities elsewhere in the world at about the same time. For example, at around the same time that the Timbuktu notables were establishing the golden age of their city in West Africa, merchant elites on the northern shores of the German empire built flourishing port cities such as Lübeck and Hamburg. As in Timbuktu, a select group of eminent families ran the trade and their municipal governments. They too eventually began to preserve their family history, often along with or as part of their family Bibles. They also were patrons of the arts and learning, although learning came to be centered in institutions quite separate from families—in universities. In contrast with surrounding monarchies, the status of a town dweller was not determined exclusively and eternally by birth. Membership in the oligarchy, or group of ruling elite families, could come and go with family fortunes. Oligarchies renewed themselves periodically with the infusion of the newly wealthy. There were clear distinctions among families, but which families belonged where in the social hierarchy could change over a few generations.

Archaeologists and historians argue that the emergence of state-centered societies in the ancient world marked an important turning point in human history. State organizations accrued wealth and resources that enabled the large-scale building projects and the administrative complexity that we associate with ancient civilizations and their cities. But as was true of older forms of human society, power relations and family relations were closely intertwined. All forms of the ancient state depended on family relations. Dynastic models elevated one familial lineage above all others; the dramatic accumulation of power and wealth that successful dynasties could command provided a basis for building temples and monuments, but often for the oppressive exercise of power as well, and for the imperial ambitions that drew and redrew world boundaries.

The quieter operation of rule by a select set of elite families in city-states or confederations typically focused on the smaller scale—the construction of a prominent mosque, as in Timbuktu, or a city hall, as in Hamburg. Their connections with the wider world operated often through the command of trade networks—in turn relying on kinship ties—linking outward from the home base. This model of connecting family and rule would also have consequences for world-historical dynamics with the intensification of global connections that began in the fifteenth century CE.

CHAPTER 4

Early Modern Families (1400–1750)

The first Christian wedding in Mexico occurred in 1526. Don Hernando, the brother of the Aztec ruler of Texcoco, and seven of his closest associates took wives in a Christian ceremony. Serving as godparents were two members of the army of Cortés, the Spanish conquistador—Alonso de Ávila and Pedro Sánchez Farfán—who were accompanied by their wives.[1] Farfán's wife was likely María Estrada, the only woman to come to the new world with Cortés; Ávila's wife was probably an Aztec woman. The Franciscan priest Diego Durán, writing a few decades later, commented on the ways in which the new ceremonies of marriage did not simply replace the old ones: "After I married some young men and women, with all the solemnity and ceremony the sacrament demands, after leaving the church, they were taken to a house of the old people and were married again, with the ancient ceremonies and rites."[2]

Renegotiations of family rituals such as this one became more frequent after around 1500, when a series of transatlantic voyages of exploration put the "Old World" (Europe, Asia, and Africa) in touch with the "New World" of the Americas. All parts of the globe soon came to be interconnected, but from the viewpoint of global family history, this connection might be thought of as a reunion of sorts, if even more dramatic, conflicted, and awkward than most family reunions. After its emergence in Africa, the human species spread across the globe. Subsequently, however, the branches of humanity living in the Eastern and Western hemispheres were effectively cut off from each other for some 15,000 years or more. After the voyages undertaken by European navigators starting with Columbus in 1492, peoples who had been living apart for millennia forged new relationships. These early modern encounters raised new questions about what it meant to be human. Sexual relations, gender identities, and family life shaped these encounters and were also the focus of cross-cultural observations and conflicts.

Ancient connections of trade and travel among the various Old World cultures of Asia, Europe, and Africa had certainly made some people aware of a variety of forms of family life even before the transatlantic voyages of the late fifteenth century. For example, in the fourteenth century the Muslim scholar Ibn Battuta left his birthplace of Tangiers to travel as a pilgrim to Mecca. He later wrote descriptions of the places he visited on this trip and subsequent ones throughout the Mediterranean and West Africa. Ibn Battuta's observations reveal much about the types of families he encountered, as well as the ideas and expectations that were the basis of his comparisons. For example, he notes of his visit to Turkey: "A remarkable thing which I saw in this country was the respect shown to women by the Turks, for they hold a more dignified position than the men . . . on leaving Qiram, I saw the wife of the amir [prince] . . . Skins of *qumizz* [curdled milk] were brought and she, pouring some into a cup, knelt before him and gave it to him, afterwards pouring out a cup for his brother. Then the amir poured out a cup for her and food was brought in and she ate with him."[3] The reciprocity of the relationship between husband and wife, and their relative equality, apparently struck Ibn Battuta as unusual.

In Walata, in western Africa, Ibn Battuta observed family and gender relations that struck him as distinctive, compared not only with his homeland but with nearly all other places: "Their men show no signs of jealousy whatever; no one claims descent from his father, but on the contrary from his mother's brother. A person's heirs are his sister's sons, not his own sons. This is a thing which I have seen nowhere in the world except among the Indians of Malabar. But those are heathens; *these* people are Muslims, punctilious in observing the hours of prayer, studying books of law, and memorizing the Koran. Yet their women show no bashfulness before men and do not veil themselves, though they are assiduous in attending the prayers."[4]

Most people were not travelers like Ibn Battuta, and his writings circulated only to a limited extent before the era of the printing press. They became widely known only when they were discovered and translated into several languages beginning in the eighteenth century. Most people of his time lived in limited cultural worlds within which local family arrangements appeared to them as natural and universal. The intensification of long-distance maritime travel that began in the early fifteenth century changed this. Travel brought awareness of new worlds, not just to those who actually traveled but also to those who bought new trade products, read the travelers' tales, or saw the images of exotic places and peoples that circulated widely by the second half of the fifteenth century in new media, such as the books and prints of images that Europe's new printing presses churned out in large numbers.

Christopher Columbus, in a letter written in 1493 to the Spanish king and queen describing his travels to "India," informed them that he had taken possession, in the name of the Spanish empire, of the island he named Hispana (now the countries of Haiti and the Dominican Republic). He briefly described the terrain and people there, noting that "both sexes in this island, and in all the others which I have seen . . . go always naked as they were born, with the exception of some of the women, who use the covering of a leaf, or small bough, or an apron of cotton which they prepare for that purpose." "As far as I have learned," Columbus noted, "in all these islands, as I understand, every man is satisfied with one wife, except the princes or kings, who are permitted to have 20. The women appear to work more than the men."[5]

Encounters like this one that occurred in the context of conquest or colonization often led to vigorous interventions in local family life. Conquerors might choose simply to adopt the customs of those they conquered, but this was rare. More typically, they attempted to alter local customs in ways that would buttress their own power, or else they tried to impose their own rules onto conquered peoples. Family alliances could serve as nodes of colonial power or of resistance to colonial rule, so it was important to empire builders to address family dynamics as part of the imposition of imperial rule.

There were prior examples of this in Old World empires such as that of the Ottoman Turks, who had expanded westward from an original base in Central Asia. During the early modern period, much of the Ottoman Empire's dramatic expansion relied on a new type of military and administrative elite—the so-called janissary system, which was in place from the late thirteenth through the early nineteenth centuries. Members of the janissary corps were recruited through the capture of young boys from Christian populations subject to the Ottoman sultan. The boys became elite slaves of the sultan, were educated at court, generally converted to Islam, and were forbidden to marry or form close ties with the populations where they served. They lived a very comfortable lifestyle in many respects, in that they were well rewarded for their service and held some of the empire's highest positions of power. However, they could not form families.

The janissary system was a deliberate strategy for creating an imperial ruling elite whose only loyalty would be to the sultan and the Ottoman state. This system allowed the sultan to circumvent the local kin and tribal alliances and family loyalties that he would have encountered had he tried to integrate local elite families into his administrative bureaucracy. Since the aim was to undercut the formation of family ties that might compete with imperial ties, the janissary system might best be described as an "anti-family" ruling strategy. The sultans' solution nevertheless represents one approach to the problem of creating a family policy that would serve the ends of empire building.

Other ruling dynasties developed different family strategies as implements of conquest. The Mughals, who began their conquest of India under Emperor Babur in the early sixteenth century, adopted a policy of tolerating local customs and practices as a part of their strategy of rule. The Mughals had a glorious ancestry of conquest. Babur was the direct descendant of the fourteenth-century conqueror Tamerlane on his father's side and of the great Mongol Chinggis Khan on his mother's side. The Mughals brought Islam to a largely Hindu India. Marriage was a primary method by which Mughal rulers and other members of the elite forged alliances with the peoples that they conquered.

The emperor Akbar, who ruled from 1556 to 1605, used marriage and an enormous harem as a way of creating alliances with local notables. Estimates of the size of his harem range from 300 to 5,000. In part, the size of his harem was intended to demonstrate his status and sexual potency. But the harem served specific political purposes as well. Akbar used marriage to form alliances with prominent local families, most of whom were Hindu. The *Ain i Akbari*, a document composed in the sixteenth century by the courtier Abu'l Fazl Allami to celebrate the reign of Akbar, clarifies the purposes of his marriages: "His Majesty forms matrimonial alliances with princes of Hindustan, and of other countries; and secures by these ties of harmony the peace of the world."[6] Akbar's many marriages both symbolized and consolidated his power over a vast and diverse empire. There is very little evidence that non-Muslim women in the imperial harem were pressured to adopt Islam. Their sons would have been raised as Mughal princes and hence as adherents to Islam, but they themselves were allowed to retain their original religions. Nor is there much evidence that the Mughal rulers were interested in converting the population at large; their vision of empire, reflected within their households, allowed for religious diversity.[7]

In contrast, the Spanish conquest of Mexico in the New World involved a very ambitious effort to substitute the Catholic faith as well as Spanish family practices for indigenous ones. The early modern European drive toward maritime expansion and colonization was led by Portugal and Spain beginning in the late fifteenth century. Not coincidentally, the domestic preparation for Spain's building of a New World empire

This lavish painting records the birth of Prince Salim, who was the son of the Mughal emperor Akbar and one of his Hindu wives, Jodha Bai. The mother is attended by a female entourage while men wait outside. Salim would assume the Mughal throne as the Emperor Jahangir in 1605. Photograph © Museum of Fine Arts, Boston; Bishandas, Indian, active about 1590–1650, *Birth of a Prince* (detail), Indian, Mughal, Mughal period, about 1620, Object Place: Northern India, Opaque watercolor and on paper, 10 3/8 × 6 1/2 in., Museum of Fine Arts, Boston, Francis Bartlett Donation of 1912 and Picture Fund, 14.657

involved political and dynastic consolidation. Spain was united under the joint rule of King Ferdinand and Queen Isabella, who had each inherited lands in different regions of Spain and whose joint territories were united by their marriage. This political consolidation reflected the notions of hereditary rule that prevailed in many regions of Europe.

The Habsburg monarchy that eventually succeeded Ferdinand and Isabella to rule Spain and much of Europe as well as Mexico in the sixteenth century was a monarchy built on careful marriage and inheritance strategies. It was also built on a tightening of the rules of the Catholic religion and a heightened emphasis on the "blood lines" through which property, power, and religious affiliations were passed down. Maritime ventures undertaken beginning in the late fifteenth century had political and religious, as well as economic, dimensions, to which Columbus refers explicitly in the prologue to his logbook:

> [In] this present year of 1492, your Highnesses concluded . . . the war with the Moors who reigned in Europe . . . and as Catholic Christians and as princes devoted to the holy Christian faith . . . and enemies of the sect of Mahomet and of all idolatries and heresies, took thought to send me, Christopher Columbus, to India, to see the princes and peoples and lands and . . . the manner which should be used to bring about their conversion to our Holy Faith.[8]

The process of conversion can be peaceful, but often it is not. The Spanish conquest of Mexico involved efforts to convert the inhabitants to Christianity, which also brought significant changes to family life, although transformations in both realms were uneven and incomplete as indigenous practices survived in altered forms.

The attempt to export Spanish rule and Christianity to Mexico was complicated by the fact that what it meant to be Christian was a subject of enormous contention in Europe precisely in this era. The specific form of Christianity exported through colonization and its impact on imperial family policies bore the imprint of European religious conflicts. The Reformation was changing the religious landscape of Europe at the same time that the Spanish were colonizing Mexico.

Launched in 1517 by the German monk Martin Luther's public criticism of the Roman Catholic Church, the ensuing religious Reformation resulted in the secession of much of northern and central Europe from the Catholic Church and the establishment of alternative churches jointly referred to as Protestant. Luther's grounds for criticizing and then leaving the Catholic Church were multiple, but his key argument was that the Church had departed from God's will as embodied in the Old and New Testament; the aim of reform was to bring Christians back to Scripture. Questions of family and sexuality were more prominent in his thinking than is generally recognized. In 1532, when Luther summarized the main goals of the reform, he gave marriage a prominent place: "The Lord God has wanted three things made right again before the Last Day: the ministry of the Word, government, and marriage."[9]

Early in his career as a reformer, in 1522, Luther preached a sermon on marriage that laid the groundwork for Lutheran reform of marriage law, like his other reforms based on the interpretation of Scripture:

> Let us direct our attention to Genesis 1[:27], 'So God created man . . . male and female he created them.' From this passage we may be assured that God divided mankind into two classes, namely, male and female . . . Therefore, each one of us must have the kind of body God has created for us. I cannot make myself a woman, nor can you make yourself a man . . . The man is not to despise or scoff at the woman or her body, nor the woman the man . . . In the second place, after God had made man and woman he blessed them and said to them, 'Be fruitful and multiply' [Gen. 1:28]. From this passage we may be assured that man and woman should and must come together in order to multiply . . . For it is not a matter of free choice or decision but a natural and necessary thing, that whatever is a man must have a woman and whatever is a woman must have a man.[10]

For Luther, marriage was the institution established by God for the expression of human sexuality; no other form of sexual relations was permissible.

Luther contested the Catholic Church's elevation of celibacy above marriage as the ideal state for a Christian. The Lutheran reformers believed that everyone should marry. Luther argued that women's "natural" sexual desire is inextricably linked to motherhood; conversely, he saw women who were not interested in marriage and motherhood as unnatural. He and his followers condemned sexuality outside of marriage for men and for women, and they attacked the Catholic practice of clerical celibacy, encouraging Protestant pastors to marry.

According to Luther, "priests, monks, and nuns are duty-bound to forsake their vows whenever they find that God's ordinance to produce seed and to multiply is powerful and strong within them . . . hinder [this ordinance], however, you may be sure that they will not remain pure but inevitably besmirch themselves with secret sins or fornication." There was one additional question for which these principles had immediate practical impact: the necessity of parental permission to marry. Lutherans rejected the pre-Reformation view of marriage as a sacrament, made valid solely by the free exchange of the marriage promise

Chör Menſch ſo du zu tiſch wilt gon
Dein hend ſolt du gewaſchen hon
Lang negel zymen auch nit wol
Die man heymlich abſchneiden ſol
Am tiſch ſetz dich nit oben an
Der haußuatter wöls dan ſelber hon
Der Benedeyung nit vergiß
Jnn Gottes nam heb an vnd iß
Den Eldiſten anſahen laß
Darnach iß züchtiglicher maß
Nit ſchnaude oder ſewiſch ſchmatz
Nit vngeſtümb nach brot platz
Das du keyn gſchyr vmbſtoſſen thuſt
Das brot ſchneid nit an deiner bruſt
Das geſchnitten brot oder weck
Nit deinen henden nit verdeck
Vnd brock nit mit den zenen eyn
Vnd greyff auch für dein orth aleyn
Thu nit in der ſchüſſel vmb ſtüren
Darob halten will nit gepüren
Den Löffel nim auch nit zu fol
Wan du draiffeſt es ſtet nit wol
Greyff auch nach keyner ſpeiſe meer
Biß dir deyn mundt ſey worden leer
Red nit mit vollem mund ſey meſſig

Sey in der ſchüſſel nit gefreſſig
Der aller letzt dann ob dem tiſch
Zerſchneid das fleyſch vnd pcich die fiſch
Vnd kewe mit verſchloſſem mund
Schlag nit die züg auß gleich ein hund
So du iſt thu nit geitzig ſchlincken
Vnd wiſch den mund ſo du wilt trincken
Das du nit ſchmalzig machſt den wein
Trinck ſülich vnd huſt nit dar ein
Thu auch nit grölzen oder kreiſten
Schüt dich auch nit vnd ſey am weiſten
Setz hälbſchlich vngeſchüret nider
Bring kein andren zu trincken wider
Füll keyn glaß mit dem andren nicht
Würff auch auff niemant dein geſicht
Als ob du merckeſt auff ſein eſſen
Wer neben dir am tiſch iß gſeſſen
Den yre nit mit dein elbogen
Sitz auffgericht fein geſchmogen
Ruck nit hin vnd her auff dem penck
Das du nit macheſt ein geſtenck
Dein füß las vnderm tiſch nit gamppern
Dar zu hüt dich vor allen ſchamppern
Wotten/nachreden/geſpöt vnd lachen
Sey erbarlich in allen ſachen

Zu pulerey laß dich nit mercken
Thu auch niemant auff hader ſtercken
Gezanck am tiſch gar übel ſtat
Sag nichts darob man grawen hat
Vnd thu dich auch am tiſch nit ſchneutz
Das andre nit vor dir thon ſcheutzen
Gee nit vmbzauſen in der naſen
Deß zanſtürens ſolt du dich maſſen
Jm kopff ſolt du dich auch nit krawen
Der gleich ſollen junckfraw vnd frawen
Nach keynem floch hinunder viſchen
Anß tiſchtuch ſoll ſich nimant wiſchen
Auch leg den kopff nit in die hent
Leyn dich nit hinden an die wendt
Biß das mal hat ſeinen auß banck
Dan ſag Gott heymlich lob vnd danck
Der dir dein ſpeiſe hat beſchert
Auß vetterlicher hant ernert
Darnach ſolt du vom tiſch auff ſten
Dein hent waſchen vnd wider geen
An dein gewerb vnd arbeyt ſchwer
So ſpricht Hans Sachs Schuchmach:
(er.

Gedruckt zu Nürnberg durch
Hanns Wandereiſen.

This woodcut of a family seated at the dinner table illustrates a poem by Hans Sachs entitled "Table Manners," published in Germany in 1534. The family uses plates and utensils and servants offer food and drink. The poem and its illustration circulated new ideals of a pious and orderly family life developed in the context of Lutheran reform. bpk, Berlin /Kupferstichkabinett, Staatliche Museen / Photo by Joerg P. Anders /Art Resource, NY

between a man and a woman. Because they viewed marriage as a status to be regulated by families and public authorities, they required that marriages be solemnized publicly with church ceremony.

But changes were not limited to Protestant areas. Christians who chose to remain Catholic, or whose rulers decided for them to maintain Roman Catholicism as the state church, also felt compelled by many of the same pressures to reform morality and to exert tighter controls over family life. The Council of Trent, which convened between 1545 and 1563, took up many questions of Catholic religious life. Its decisions had consequences for the family life of Catholics not just in Europe but also throughout those regions of the world affected by colonization by Catholic European states or by Christian missionary efforts, which expanded in the wake of the Catholic Reform.

One of the key areas addressed at the Council of Trent was marriage. In the face of new Protestant views, the Catholic Church continued to hold celibacy as practiced by monks and nuns in higher esteem than marriage. But discipline over priests, monks, and nuns was tightened so as to rectify and prevent the moral abuses that had been part of the rationale for the Reformation. Of particular relevance for women, all female convents were brought under male authority and the lives of religious women who chose to become nuns were constrained in new ways. Convents were cloistered—that is, sealed off from routine direct contact with the secular world.

The Catholic Church also increased its control over the sacrament of marriage through its requirement that marriages be announced and recorded in the parish church and witnessed by the priest, but the Church also reinforced the old proviso that, as a Christian sacrament, marriage could not be forced upon someone against his or her will. This rule of course set up the Church in opposition to parental power over children in marital choices. Church courts claimed authority to adjudicate disputes among family members—usually between parents and children—over decisions about marriage. In practice, this could mean that young people could go to a Church court if they were pressured into a marriage they did not want. For example, in 1556, the Church's matrimonial court in Bologna dispensed Diamante Nanni, then thirteen years old, from a promise of marriage to Alessandro Totti, who was twelve years older than her. The court's investigation revealed that the betrothal had been negotiated between the fathers of Diamante and Alessandro, when Diamante was just eight years old, in a failed attempt to end a feud between the two families. Diamante's own testimony played an important role in the deliberations. She made it clear to the court that she had not consented to the betrothal and "knew nothing about this promise until the ring was handed over." Moreover, she also explained to the court that she had resisted Alessandro's efforts to consummate the marriage on two occasions following the betrothal.[11]

The Catholicism that was exported to Mexico was this Catholicism of the Catholic Counter-Reformation, of the Council of Trent. The Catholic Church and the Spanish state were partners in the conquest of Mexico, as they were in the rule over Spain itself. Both Church and state had interests in bringing new rules governing marriage and the family to Mexico. Of course, the relative ease of the Spanish and Catholic political and cultural conquest is explained in great measure by the demographic catastrophe that the Spaniards brought to the indigenous people. The population of the area that was to become known as New Spain plummeted from a preconquest high of perhaps ten to twelve million people to 750,000 in the early seventeenth century.[12] Some of the deaths were due to warfare, but more were due to new diseases to which the native populations had no immunity.

In the aftermath of this disaster, the Spanish imposed a new regime and a new family system simultaneously. Rules about marriage that had been developed in the context of Reformation-era Catholic Europe were introduced into Mexico, where they met with some success. Prior to the Conquest, there had been a great variety in Indian marriage practices, but in general marriages among cousins were common, and men might have more than one wife. A man's status was often reflected in the number of his wives; the Aztec ruler Moctezuma, who ruled from 1502 to 1520, for example, supposedly had several hundred concubines in addition to his two legal wives. The Spanish colonial rulers enacted legal codes in Mexico based on Catholic Church and Spanish laws as early as the sixteenth century. For example, the Church introduced Christian rules about consanguinity (that is, blood relationship), which spelled out prohibitions against cousin marriages. Even more important, the church tried to eliminate concubinage and polygamy. These laws reflected Christian views of family morality.

Although the Mexican Church and colonial state were remarkably successful in converting the population of New Spain to at least nominal Catholicism, changes in marriage practices seem to have succeeded far more among the urban upper classes than in rural areas. The vast majority of the thousands of Spaniards who came to New Spain in the course of the sixteenth and seventeenth centuries were men. Some of these men married women from wealthy families, thereby acquiring access to land or other forms of wealth. These intermarried families formed a political and economic elite that generally followed Spanish customs. The Hinojosa family of Cuernavaca was able to maintain its networks of influence in indigenous society while promoting and extending its political and economic authority through marriages with Spaniards.[13]

The complexity of marriage arrangements can be seen in the example of don Antonio Hinojosa. The title don reflects status as a Spaniard; don Antonio was also referred to as "son of a tlatoani [indigenous elite]." In 1656, he married doña Felipe de Haro Bravo y San Román; her father was a Spaniard and her mother was a member of the indigenous elite. Their children were recorded in a "Book of Spaniards."[14]

Officially, monogamous marriage sanctioned by the Church displaced the earlier practices. However, among ordinary people and in rural areas, couples (even those who were in other ways practicing Catholics) would often live in consensual unions, which were not recognized by the church as marriage but were rooted in previous marital forms involving cohabitation during a long period of bride service, a practice in which the husband would provide labor for the bride's family. So, although the new family system was by no means fully established by the end of the sixteenth century, or even later, the family dimensions of colonial ruling strategy are apparent.

Early modern colonization brought distinct ways of organizing families into contact and often conflict with one another. Much was at stake, ranging from understandings of morality and religious practice to social status and the orderly transmission of property and power, through the symbolic power of family relations to mirror and reinforce political relations of authority. But in the early modern world of "first encounters," something else was also at stake—namely, basic notions of categorizing people into groups. Intermarriages and other sexual unions across different systems called into question older systems of categorization.

The historical roots of modern notions of race as a particular form of categorization are deep and complex. European scientific notions about race did not fully develop until the nineteenth century. Certainly, part of the story of the development of the concept of race is to be found in the hardening of racial differences that resulted from the African slave trade that flourished in the wake of the establishment of plantation economies in the New World. But marriage and other sexual unions between colonizers and colonized, and the offspring those relationships produced, significantly contributed to the ways in which racial categories were developed historically.

Español con India.
Mestizo.

Mestizo con Española.
Castizo.

Castizo con Española.
Español.

Español con Mora.
Mulato.

5

6

7

Mulato con Española.
Morisco.

Morisco con Española.
Chino.

Chino con India.
Salta atras.

Salta atras con Mulata.
Lobo.

9

10

11

12

Lobo con China.
Gibaro.

Gibaro con Mulata.
Albarazado.

Albarazado con Negra.
Canbujo.

Canbujo con India.
Sanbaigo.

13

14

15

16

Sanbaigo con Loba.
Calpamulato.

Calpamulato con Canbuja.
Tente en elAire.

Tente enelAire con Mulata.
Note entiendo.

Noteentiendo con India.
Tornaatras.

This series of sixteen casta *(caste) paintings represents the offspring of intermarriages in colonial Mexico. The first painting, in the upper left hand corner, shows that a marriage between a Spanish man and an Indian woman results in a Mestizo child. The sixteenth and final painting shows a union between a man characterized as "No te entiendo" (literally meaning "I don't understand you") and an Indian woman, as producing a child described as a "Torna atras" (turns back). These paintings were very common in eighteenth-century Mexico: the categorizations they used were not always identical, but they show a concern with mapping the results of intermarriages.* Schalkwijk /Art Resource, NY

The earliest groupings Europeans used to describe the peoples they encountered on transatlantic voyages were drawn according to a variety of models. Some voyagers simply took accounts from myths or older travel reports and substituted new place names. These descriptions typically wavered between acknowledging a common humanity with newly encountered people and describing customs or appearances that denigrated non-Europeans as "barbarous" or "un-Christian" and thus inferior to the European observer. This was true in the way Columbus described the indigenous peoples he saw. In a similar manner, Amerigo Vespucci, writing at the end of the 1490s about his encounters with people in the Americas, included observations about physical traits, such as body hair, but also comments on cultural habits and daily life. He asserted, for example, that their mode of life "is very barbarous, for they have no regular time for their meals, but they eat at any time that they have the wish."[15]

During the period of early modern encounters there is evidence of new notions about the nature of differences among peoples. Some of these differences began to appear as innate and biologically transmissible—that is, "racial" distinctions. Initially, Spaniards had talked about differences among people in terms of *casta*, a Spanish word meaning "caste" or "estate." This word refers to legal and occupational distinctions, often hereditary. In fifteenth-century Spain, the emphasis on lineage elements of social distinction was intensified for political reasons. The triumph of royal rule that Ferdinand and Isabella established with their union of the Spanish monarchy in 1492 emphasized the principle of dynastic lineages. Moreover, their consolidation of power and their alliance with Catholicism entailed more rigidly distinguishing between Catholics of long lineage or "pure blood" and politically and religiously suspect groups such as Jews, Muslims, and recent converts to Catholicism. Both of these political developments called attention to family lineage.

In the Mexican colonial context, *casta* took on new meanings, referring to all the people of Mexico who were not of "pure" Spanish heritage. In the colonial Mexican society, the mix also included new peoples—indigenous Americans and African slaves. It became common practice by the eighteenth century to see and record status categories that included what might be called racial dimensions (skin color and other physical attributes) as well as family lineage and social status markers. Although the early intermarriages among Spaniards and indigenous peoples were the basis of the emergent colonial elite in the sixteenth century, by the eighteenth century carefully categorizing the offspring of such marriages was of increasing interest. A very specific new genre—*casta* paintings—popularized this evolving system of categorization.

The *casta* paintings ranked intermarried couples and their offspring according to an elaborate system including dimensions of social status, physical attributes, occupation, and wealth. They depicted families who were closer to "pure Spanish" blood as better off, better dressed, lighter skinned, and living in cleaner and more comfortable surroundings. Of course, these paintings cannot be read as ethnographic records of actual conditions. Rather, they represent an imagined ordering of the social hierarchy along newly racialized lines that appealed to the ruling classes of eighteenth-century Mexico. The paintings focus on a large and complex set of new categories of people that continually emerge through unions across the varying types of people who encountered each other in Mexico. Although they do not portray race as a binary or even fixed category, the paintings do suggest that race consciousness and its connections with status were beginning to be codified.

The dramatic transformations associated with the early modern intensification of global encounters—navigation, exploration, trade, religious proselytization, conquest, and colonization—shaped and were shaped by family life and family ideals. Conquering imperial rulers had to decide either to form alliances through marriage or collaboration with conquered lineages or kin groups, or else to replace them with alternative lineages or forms of rule designed to circumvent family power. New, often hybrid, religious practices and new ideas about categories of people and their relationships to one another (such as were embodied in emerging notions of race) also drew from family practices and relied upon family metaphors. The dramatic encounters that shaped global-historical dynamics of the early modern era were simultaneously, inescapably, family encounters as well.

CHAPTER 5

Families in Global Markets (1600–1850)

A key moment in Charles Dickens's *A Christmas Carol* (1843) occurs during Christmas dinner in the home of the Cratchit family: "Mrs. Cratchit entered: flushed but smiling proudly: with the pudding . . . blazing in ignited brandy, and bedight with Christmas holly stuck into the top." In 1850, Dickens's friend Charles Knight wrote a story about Christmas pudding for the popular British periodical *Household Words*. In it he listed a recipe for this traditional English holiday dessert: "One pound raisins; one pound currants; one pound suet; one pound breadcrumbs; quarter pound orange peel; one nutmeg; one teaspoonful powdered cinnamon; one wineglassful brandy; seven eggs; one teaspoonful salt; quarter pound raw sugar . . ."[1] In earlier centuries the pudding had been simpler, but by Dickens's time a proper pudding required ingredients from all over the globe, as Knight's article made explicit. The raisins, currants, and oranges came from various points in the Mediterranean; nutmeg found its way from the so-called Spice Islands of Indonesia, then part of the Dutch Empire; cinnamon came from Ceylon and raw sugar from the West Indies.

Foods prepared for families were changing around the world as a result of the global trade explosion of the early modern era. "New World crops" like yams, potatoes, and corn had altered diets throughout the Old World in the centuries after 1492; they did so by being introduced into local crop rotations in Europe, Asia, and Africa. In contrast, many of the newly popular agricultural products could not be locally grown and had to be imported. Coffee drinking moved, slowly at first, from Ethiopia to Arabia, Egypt, and the Ottoman Empire; it leapt to Italy in the sixteenth century and from there spread rapidly through European cities. European appetites for coffee and tea, like appetites for spices, could be met only through importation from warmer regions. By the seventeenth century, the market for other basic commodities, many of which were used for clothing—such as cotton, silk, and flax—was also "going global" at an accelerated rate.

The historical forces that fed into the English Christmas pudding recipe and other exotic products connected families across the globe in very different ways. The Cratchits and their real-life counterparts purchased exotic products; these products came to figure in images of ideal family life that originated in Europe's wealthy urban classes but became more widespread toward the end of the eighteenth century through popular publications like novels, family magazines, and household advice books.

However, the new products had begun entering the ports and market baskets of Europe long before Dickens wrote *A Christmas Carol*, as a result of the work of networks of global merchants. Traders in the new commodities often did business through networks built on family ties; when they set up trade bases across the globe, they either brought their immediate families with them or built new ones, forging closer connections with local populations. Merchants relied upon trusted members of their extended family networks in faraway places for merchandise, credit, and political advice. To offer just one example, when the young Portuguese merchant Luis Suarez arrived in the West Indies in 1634 to launch his career, his family connections served as a recommendation for him, as is clear from the letter that one local merchant wrote to another announcing Suarez's arrival: "In this fleet arrived the son of Fernando Fernandes Ribeiro, nephew and son-in-law of Antonio Nuñez Gramaxo. . . . He plans to establish his house here. . . . I have heard that he is a capable person of great consideration, in sum: the true disciple of Antonio Nuñez Gramaxo."[2]

A more ominous development related to expanding global trade involved the disruption and reorganization of labor. To meet market demand in Europe and elsewhere, merchant entrepreneurs established plantations based on slave labor; the brutal slave trade that ensued in turn turned people into a commodity—something that could be bought and sold—and uprooted millions of people, especially West Africans, from home and family. Even on farms that did not employ slave labor, the commercialization of agriculture altered family forms and reorganized traditional farm family life throughout Eurasia and elsewhere in the world. In the early modern commercial revolution that produced the global marketplace, business and family transformation were inseparable.

Armenian merchants were vital to the early modern development of global trade based on networks of family and business relationships.

They had long been important figures in the overseas and Mediterranean trade that linked Asia, North Africa, and Europe. But by the early seventeenth century, political rivalries on the border of the Ottoman and Safavid empires created a situation that dramatically altered the role of Armenian merchants in world trade. The Armenian town of Julfa was destroyed in 1604, and, in the aftermath of Safavid victories, the emperor forced the Armenian merchant community to move more than 1,000 kilometers southeastward to New Julfa, a newly built suburb of the Safavid capital of Isfahan. This relocation represented a deliberate strategy to enrich and strengthen the Safavid state through the wealth that Armenian traders could be expected to bring in.

An Armenian trade colony was set up in New Julfa; the Armenian community was given special status, privileges, and monopolies, and eventually New Julfa became the center of an international network of Armenian merchant enterprises. From their new base, the reach of Armenian trade communities extended all the way from Paris into the eastern Indian Ocean. The organizational base upon which Armenian trade success was built went far beyond mere trade. The links that tied far-flung Armenian communities together—for trust and credit were critical to long-distance maritime trade—were links of kinship, language, business practices, and a special form of Christianity, which preserved Armenians' shared identity and shared sense of distinctiveness and trust.[3]

Family connections were also at the core of the processes by which the Sephardic Jewish diaspora produced the world's first "global enterprises." (Sephardic Jews trace their origins to the Iberian Peninsula.) In the 1530s, Beatrice Mendes, the young widow of a wealthy Portuguese merchant, fled from Lisbon to Antwerp. Her brother-in-law Diego Mendes, a spice merchant then living in Antwerp, was using his many contacts across Europe to help resettle family members and friends who, like Beatrice, were being persecuted because they were Jews or *conversos*—that is, descendants of Jews who had been forced to convert to Christianity but who were always under suspicion of practicing Judaism in the privacy of their family life.

Beatrice invested her family fortune in her brother-in-law's business, and she eventually became an adept businesswoman herself. After her brother-in-law's death, she moved herself, her daughter, and a considerable household to Venice. Beatrice relocated in Venice because in the 1540s the city-state welcomed Jews and *conversos* and offered them a safe base from which to conduct the commercial enterprises upon which both the merchant families' and the city's fortunes rested. In Italy she traded successfully in pepper, grain, and textiles.[4]

When political conditions for Jews changed in Venice, the Mendes household moved again, along with their substantial family business capital, first to Ferrara and then to Istanbul in the Ottoman Empire. Ambassadorial records show the extent to which Beatrice's personal and business plans and travels were of interest to the international community. Hearing rumors of her planned departure from his city, the French ambassador in Venice wrote home in 1549 that a special envoy had been sent from the Ottoman sultan in Constantinople to ask the Venetians "to hand over to him the Portuguese, Mendes, together with her daughter and her property, to take them with him to Constantinople. Rumor has it that the said Mendes has married her daughter, or promised her, to the son of a certain Hamon, a Jew, physician to the Grand Signior [that is, the sultan], who favors him more than any other person of his own creed." The ambassador added that this development made clear what had long been suspected of Mendes, that "she and all her tribe has been and is one of the sect of the Marranos [a term referring to Portuguese *conversos*], having pretended to be Christian, in order to become rich by trading freely with all the merchants."[5]

Beatrice Mendes's travels were part of a larger diaspora that drove Jews from their homes in Spain and Portugal to cities across the globe beginning at the close of the fifteenth century. (In this context, "diaspora" refers to the migration of a group, either voluntarily or involuntarily, to a great geographic expanse from a common point of origin.) The diaspora created global family and business networks. Among the many diasporic merchant communities that have played a role in world history, the networks of Sephardic Jews (that is, Jews of Spanish or Portuguese origin) were the widest-ranging. They linked commerce in the Mediterranean with the Indian Ocean and eventually the New World. Ties of kinship, repeated intermarriages, and a common experience of religious persecution connected traders with one another across wide distances and over generations. These family and religious loyalties and relations of trust took priority over political affiliations, which made this group mobile and flexible, on the one hand, but politically vulnerable, on the other.

The Jewish trade diaspora from the Iberian Peninsula, notable for its truly global scope based on family ties, began in the late 1400s. As a culmination of the consolidation of power of the Spanish monarchy, Jewish families who had long lived in Spain were forced to convert or leave. Since they were already in the business of trade and money lending in Spain, Portugal, and elsewhere in the Mediterranean basin, the Sephardim extended their trade networks as they scattered throughout the

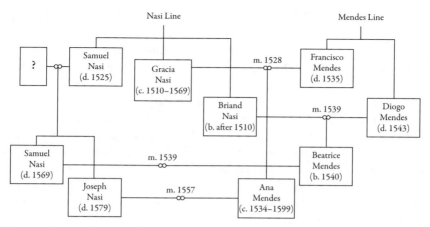

This family tree illustrates how marriages were a strategy for linking Sephardic Jewish merchant families and their wealth across generations. The double sibling marriages that connected the Mendes family and the Nasi family in both genera-tions. The genealogical research represented by family trees such as this one is a useful tool for analyzing family-historical dynamics. Data from Mariam Bodian, "Doña Gracia Nasi," Jewish Women's Archive, **http://jwa.org/encylopedia/ article/nasi-dona-gracia** *(downloaded August 13, 2009)*

world. They traveled not only to commercial centers of Italy and Prot-estant Northern Europe like Antwerp, Amsterdam, and London, but, like Beatrice Mendes, even farther afield to the Ottoman Empire or to India. Eventually, family branches established themselves in the New World as well.

Sephardic communities formed globally networked enclaves wher-ever they went. They took advantage of their tenuous position to act as economic go-betweens and cultural intermediaries; unlike most of their contemporaries, their family relationships even cut across religious communities, as some branches remained Jewish (openly or secretly) and some converted to Christianity. The da Costa family, originally traders and glassmakers in the city of León in northern Spain, main-tained ties among family members who had made different strategic choices in moments of religious persecution. Some, such as the mer-chant Alexander da Costa, converted to Christianity and stayed in Spain, although like many other so-called New Christians he was sus-pected of being secretly Jewish. His business ties with Jewish merchants were based on family trust, but they could cause suspicion among his Christian co-religionists. Abram da Costa de León left Spain and moved to the Italian port city of Genoa in the mid-fifteenth century, where he persuaded the city to lift its ban against Jews and allow Sephardic refugees to settle. He openly practiced Judaism.

Other da Costas relocated in London and Amsterdam. James da Costa was a wealthy international trader who helped found one of Amsterdam's first synagogues in the early seventeenth century. In the mid-seventeenth century, the *converso* Benjamin da Costa and several other members of the family were involved in launching the New World sugar industry, first on plantations in Brazil and later, after they were forced out of Brazil, in the French and Dutch West Indies. Family ties that transmitted kinship, shared history, wealth, and trust were critical to the da Costas' survival and success. They forged the bonds that were the basis of the earliest global enterprises. Their family business enterprises even embroiled them in international political intrigues, for example, the seventeenth-century trade wars between the Dutch and the Spaniards in the Caribbean. Spanish Inquisition records mention two da Costas—Lope de Acosta Suarez and David de Acosta—who were helping the Dutch as spies who were "responsible for the capture of many ships & other things."[6]

In cities around the world where they settled, the Sephardim often lived in complex households that were the basis of both family and business life. These households might include near and distant kin, apprentices, and employees. Historians estimate that there were hundreds of Sephardic households created by the diaspora, whose networks crossed the globe. For example, in the early 1600s, the merchant Manuel Bautista's household in Lima (in Peru) included Manuel Bautista himself, his wife Guiomar, their three children, his sister-in-law Isabel, and her husband Sebastian Duarte, plus two other in-laws and five cousins.[7]

Any one of these merchant households had ties with numerous others. For example, in the mid-1600s, the members of the merchant household of the Silveira family based in Cartagena de Indias (in what is now Colombia) had close business ties to branches of their family in Guinea (in West Africa), Lisbon (in Portugal), Madrid (in Spain), Goa (in South Asia), Malacca (in Malaysia), Macao (near China), and Nagasaki (in Japan). These ties across the boundaries of religion and empire contributed to the ability of these families to accumulate great mercantile fortunes. At the same time, however, the secrecy and clannishness that was necessary and intrinsic to the Sephardic family and business culture also meant that Sephardim were often suspected of political disloyalty, whether or not they converted and whether or not they adapted to local customs.

Not all merchants followed the same kinds of strategies. The different types of families that merchants founded held implications for their effectiveness and vulnerability as agents of global economic history. Sephardic Jewish and Armenian merchant communities tended to intensify their relationships, protect their religious practices, and concentrate capital by keeping their marital alliances within a small set of extended families. Other merchant groups followed different patterns.

On the western shores of the Indian Ocean, East African peoples created business and family connections with traders from the north who had been navigating up and down the Swahili Coast since late in the first millennium CE. Through shared settlements and intermarriage, inhabitants of trading towns along the Swahili Coast had established an economy and culture that reflected their mixed Bantu (African) and Arabic origins. Oral history traditions dating back to the fifteenth century or earlier and often written down in the eighteenth or nineteenth century describe the origins of these cities as sagas of family union. The central metaphor of these origin myths is typically a marriage between a foreign trader from the north and a local king's daughter. The following excerpt from one such origin story—about the coastal city of Kilwa—offers an example:

> Then came Sultan Ali bin Selimani, that is, the Persian. He came with his ship, and brought his goods and his children . . . They disembarked at Kilwa . . . went to the headman of the country, the elder Mrimba, and asked for a place in which to settle . . . This they obtained, and they gave Mrimba presents of trade goods and beads . . . Sultan Ali married Mrimba's daughter. He lived on good terms with the people . . . Sultan Ali had a child by Mrimba's daughter, a son, who was called Sultan Mohamed bin Sultan Ali. He lived at home until he reached manhood, and then set off and went . . . to visit his grandfather, the Elder Mrimba. When he arrived, his grandfather handed over his power to him, his grandson.[8]

The origin of political authority was thus directly linked to the fusion of two families from two different regions—one who had ruled on land and one who came by sea to trade. The accompanying exchange of wealth cemented the bargain and formed the basis of rule. Family social status and political position and rituals of family life and of rule in these coastal towns continued to reinforce the links among maritime trade and the wealth it brought, family lineage, and political power. Elite families governed the coastal towns and islands and set up the warehouses and exchanges that were necessary for long-distance trade.

Trade built and relied on still other family types further east in the Indian Ocean basin. The first maritime explorers in this region were Chinese traders. While most stayed relatively close to home, operating in the islands off the coast of Southeast Asia, by the early fifteenth century some Chinese navigators ventured further west. They used Arabic maps and travelers' tales as their guides, and followed the Indian Ocean coastline from China to India and Africa. Although they collected "tribute" consisting of local products of some value, the most important aspect of tribute collection was to demonstrate and enhance the legitimacy and international prestige of the Chinese emperor. These Chinese maritime expeditions were thus distinct from the European expeditions that would come later; religious conversion and colonizing were not what motivated these early Chinese voyagers.

Nor did the expeditions convince the Chinese emperors that long-distance trade was a desirable means of enhancing wealth. Indeed, in the mid-fifteenth century the Chinese emperor banned most overseas travel by Chinese for about a century. This ban did not stop the overseas trade that had been going on for centuries, but it did change the conditions under which Chinese merchants traded. Because of the ban, Chinese merchants—virtually all of whom were men—who left China found it difficult to return, because on their return they would have been subject to penalties for leaving. Chinese merchants thus tended to settle more or less permanently in Indian Ocean ports throughout Southeast Asia, Malaysia, Indonesia, and the Philippines.

A new style of family evolved in the overseas Chinese trade communities. The merchants tended to intermarry with local women even after the Imperial ban on trade was lifted. According to a sixteenth-century Dutch traveler to the Javanese pepper market of Banten: "The Chinese live at Banten in their own quarter, which is surrounded with a strong palisade . . . When they first come from China, like other merchants they buy a wife, who serves them until they again return to China, when they again sell her, taking the children with them that they have produced. Those who live here are the ones who buy up pepper from the farmers, going through the countryside with their scales in hand . . . gathering the pepper against the return of the Chinese ships."[9]

Although this description may be accurate for some Chinese merchants living abroad, it may have been the result of the Dutchman's misunderstanding of local marriage systems. In Java, women exercised a great deal of autonomy in sexual matters (in contrast with both Europe and China); for example, a bride-price was given by the groom's family to the wife or her family at the time of a marriage (rather than the dowry given by the bride's family in Europe and China). In any event, many Chinese merchants set up more permanent families than this description would imply. Most children from these unions stayed in the islands and ports of Southeast Asia, creating families that combined Chinese and local features. Chinese fathers perpetuated Confucian traditions that emphasized the father's lineage and surname and thus fostered a "Chinese" family identity—at least in terms of family names—regardless of their wives' origins. But family food, clothing, and language often came more from the mother's culture.

By the eighteenth century, as a result of these unions, there were large communities of "Straits Chinese" people based in the straits (narrow channels) among the many islands of Malaysia. Straits Chinese maintained an identity and family culture that was distinct from those of both China and local Malaysian communities. Kinship networks were crucial in establishing and expanding trade networks. Brothers often set up shop in different parts of the Malay Peninsula; trading connections followed kin connections. Adoption of sons (and sometimes of brothers) was used as a way of cementing trade ties.

Until the mid-nineteenth century, because very few women migrated from China to Malaysia, Chinese merchants continued to found families with local women. (Indeed, some merchants maintained two families; one "at home" in China and one in Malaysia.) In general, the male offspring of these marriages were sent to China to be educated. Often the daughters of Malay women and Chinese men would be married to immigrant Chinese men. In the 1890s, a Malay Chinese wrote that the arrival of Chinese ships generated considerable interest, since they brought "welcome batches of eligible sons-in-law for the daughters who could not marry the natives of the country."[10]

After Chinese women began arriving in Malaysia in the mid-nineteenth century, the rate of marriage between Chinese men and Malay women decreased. Malay Chinese spoke a language, sometimes called Baba Malay, which was structurally Malay but which contained many Chinese words. They were thus distinct from the people of both their Chinese homeland and their country of residence. The relative success and persistence of the "Chinese" merchant communities compared with the Japanese in this same region are due to the fact that Japanese merchants, who also married local women, assimilated more fully into the communities into which they moved because they did not maintain the strong practices of patrilineage that characterized the Chinese merchants' families.[11]

The search for profits from the increasing market demand, especially in Europe, for products such as coffee, tea, and cotton that could be grown only in warm climates led merchant entrepreneurs to follow

In this 1598 Dutch engraving, a Chinese merchant (left) and his Javanese wife (center) greet a trader who brought pepper from inland cultivators (right). The marriage of Chinese men to local women was a strategy frequently used by Chinese traders to develop relationships with local economies in Southeast Asia. From Lodewycksz, *'Teerste boek—Historie van Indien,* 1598, Collection of the James Ford Bell Library, University of Minnesota

a variety of strategies. As the demand for commodities increased, one obvious response was to seek ways to increase the supply. As a result, many merchant families and networks invested or participated in state-chartered trade companies that either brought them trade monopolies over certain products within a colonial empire or else involved them directly in colonial plantations in the New World or the Indian Ocean that were established to produce such goods as sugar, spices, coffee, and tea. The da Costa family, for example, was part of a trade company that moved from trading in the New World to raising and selling Brazilian sugarcane. Coffee was another high-demand crop that moved into plantation production. Seeing the high profits made in Cairo by the coffee trade coming into Europe from East Africa and the Middle East, Dutch and English merchants got involved in the business by the seventeenth century. By the beginning of the eighteenth century, Dutch mercantile groups had established coffee plantations in Java for the European market. The French soon followed suit in their colonies in the West Indies.[12]

Merchants worked with or as planters, thus developing a new commercial agricultural sector economy based on chattel slavery. Although historians cannot make precise calculations about the scope of enslavement, they agree that between the sixteenth and the nineteenth centuries more than ten million captured Africans were taken to the Western Hemisphere to work as slaves on New World plantations.[13] Those enslaved suffered the most direct and severe consequences, but slave taking also devastated the regions and the people they left behind, mainly in West and Central Africa.

Although both men and women were taken as slaves, slave captives were disproportionately young men, since their labor was the most valuable to New World plantation owners. A letter written in 1526 to the King of Portugal by Nzinga Mbemba, the King of Kongo, complains about the impact of Portuguese merchants in Kongo:

> [M]any of our people, keenly desirous as they are of the wares and things of your Kingdoms, which are brought here by your people, and in order to satisfy their voracious appetite, seize many of our people, freed and exempt men, and very often it happens that they kidnap even noblemen and the sons of noblemen, and our relatives, and take them to be sold to the white men who are in our Kingdoms . . .[14]

African communities such as Kongo experienced repeated personal sufferings at the loss of their family members. Moreover, the disproportionate enslavement of young men meant ongoing problems for local families in areas of widespread slave raiding. Skewed sex ratios and impoverishment through the loss of labor made it difficult for new families to be established. Burdens on women increased in the communities from which men were taken.

Slaves who arrived on plantations in the Americas—if they survived the grueling passage from Africa—attempted to rebuild some form of family life and kin relationships despite the difficulties of the dehumanizing conditions of slavery and plantation life. Some plantation owners in the North American South allowed slaves to form families because they saw this as necessary on moral or religious grounds, but also because they wanted to encourage reproduction among their slaves. It was cheaper, they figured, to count on slaves' children for their future labor force than to buy new slaves. Where permitted, slaves did marry, often in churches. But slave marriage vows created questions in the minds of slaves and planters: How could persons who could be bought and sold take a solemn oath in a church to remain together "until death do us part"? Sometimes the phrase "until death or distance do us part" was used instead, signaling the precarious nature of the union.

But some slaves did form family bonds, despite the difficulties. There is evidence of these bonds in naming practices, which emphasized maternal relatives over paternal relatives. Slave memoirs are a good source for evidence about slave family life. For example, Harriet Jacobs, a slave born in North Carolina in 1818, describes close family relationships in her memoirs. She is always aware of the tenuous nature of family life, describing her grandmother as "a mother who could not call her children her own."[15]

The threat of sale was always a possibility for slaves. In some states, Louisiana, for example, it was against the law for a plantation owner to separate children younger than ten from their mothers. However, the legal system rarely interfered with the rights of planters to do as they wished with their slaves. Moreover, female slaves were always vulnerable to sexual attacks by male slave owners. Sexual relations between white planters and their slaves created families. Jacobs provides a poignant vignette of such a situation:

> I once saw two beautiful children playing together. One was a fair white child; the other was her slave, and also her sister. When I saw them embracing each other, and heard their joyous laughter, I turned sadly away from the lovely sight. I foresaw the inevitable blight that would fall on the little slave's heart. I knew how soon her laughter would be changed to sighs.[16]

Once the children reached adulthood, race and servile status would trump merely biological kinship.

In the Caribbean and in Brazil, where mortality rates among slaves were considerably higher than on North American plantations, even a semblance of family life was almost impossible. Most plantation owners seem to have reckoned that it was cheaper to keep importing new slaves from Africa than to create the kinds of conditions necessary for slaves to found families and have children.

Agriculture based on slave plantations developed primarily in European colonies in the New World and the Eastern Indian Ocean. However, the rising demand for agricultural products contributed to new types of farms in other world regions as well. On the eastern rim of the Indian Ocean, wealthy merchants of southern Arabia had begun, by the seventeenth century, to establish a plantation regime attuned to the expanding world demand for products such as dates and spices. Soon they, too, were relying heavily on slave labor, in this case largely slaves captured along East African caravan routes.

This new form of slavery was to some extent built upon older traditions of slavery in Islamic lands. Under Islamic law, slave concubines

This post–Civil War certificate from Johnston County, North Carolina, officially registered a relationship of cohabitation between two emancipated slaves that had begun nine years earlier, under slavery. Former slaves had the right to marry only after emancipation. The Heritage Center, Johnston County, North Carolina

were required to be freed upon their master's death if they had borne him children. The children of free fathers were deemed free, even if their mother was a slave. Thus servitude was not a perpetual and inheritable status as it was under the form of slavery practiced in the Americas. Nevertheless, the new forms of slavery that resulted from the expansion of commercial plantation agriculture in the eastern Indian Ocean were far more brutal than many earlier slave systems in the region had been.

Slave labor was preferred by owners of the commercial plantations on the rims of the Atlantic and Indian Oceans, but landowners, small farmers, and merchants also reorganized rural labor forces in Europe in response to the growth of a market for agricultural commodities.

Around 1500, most farming in Central and Western Europe was relatively small in scale and based on family farms. Farm families produced grains and other crops for their own subsistence (that is, to feed themselves) as well as some for limited local markets. Many European farmers were peasants who did not own land outright. Peasant households often owed rents in labor, in kind, or in cash to an aristocratic landlord. But heads of peasant families often did have the right to keep the land within the family and to determine who would inherit the right to farm their plots. So access to farms (like access to political power and mercantile wealth) was transmitted mainly through family inheritance.

Marrying and starting a family were, in turn, tied to inheriting land and other forms of farm goods and equipment like tools or animals. Such property was closely guarded, and its transmission was often spelled out in great detail in written contracts that were part of a marriage negotiation. In European peasant families, both sons and daughters could expect to inherit from their parents, but not necessarily the same forms of property. Typically, in many parts of Europe, unless there were no male heirs, land passed primarily through sons. Movable farm capital—household equipment as well as cows and other livestock—more often went to the daughters. A couple who wanted to marry would do so only when they were set up through inheritance or dowry with a farm, very often in a home of their own.

The necessity of demonstrating to the community that a young couple had what was necessary to set up a new household is reflected in customs like the bridal procession. In areas of Germany the *Brautwagen*—bridal wagon—carried the bride and her dowry goods from her village to her new home. Notarial documents and family records list the wagon's contents, often in great detail. For example, one early-eighteenth-century listing of the contents of a *Brautwagen* in Diepholz, Germany, begins with "a bedcover with 10 pounds of feathers" and ends with "six pigs," whose individual values were specified.[17] The dowry—which, with the land that so often came from the groom's side, formed the economic basis of the new household— was on display for everyone to see.

Village customs of many sorts figured into keeping farmlands and families in balance and keeping population growth slow. Since marriage in much of Central, Western, and Northern Europe was late by world-historical standards—men married in their late twenties or early thirties and women in their mid to late twenties—and births outside of marriage were relatively uncommon prior to the end of the eighteenth century, the regulation of sexuality among unmarried but sexually mature young people in this precontraceptive era was the focus of considerable

This early-twentieth-century illustration depicts the German rural custom of publicly transporting a bride's dowry goods from her home village to that of her new husband. People who lived in the area could view the possessions the bride brought into the marriage. This custom was a mechanism for community supervision of marital matches. Private collection

community attention. Often, one approach to regulating sexual unions was to make the youth of any village community effectively the morals police. Organized youth groups ran the dances and festivals where young people met. They along with their elders watched over emerging relationships to assure that those who paired up were appropriate matches in terms of the land or wealth they could expect to inherit and that they would not create families that were burdens on the village. Organized groups of young men also punished sexual miscreants with shaming rituals or nighttime serenades under the windows of those suspected of misbehavior. In short, customs like these kept many forms of youthful sexuality under control by stipulating and regulating who was allowed to do what, when, and with whom.

But the system was ridden with tensions between generations as well as between men and women and wealthy and poor families. Rising land costs and high demand for agricultural products enriched some peasant households but impoverished those whose farms were marginal. In densely settled regions of peasant agriculture such as the Rhineland and Switzerland, merchants hired poorer peasants to work in "putting out" handicraft production of textiles and other goods. Under this system, merchants advanced raw materials such as wool to rural households whose members would then work them up into finished products for sale by the merchant. State authorities throughout Central Europe encouraged entrepreneurs to establish rural putting-out industries. In some cases, officials established state-run "manufactories"— large-scale handicraft workshops—for the production of luxury goods such as porcelain, tobacco, and silk to sell on regional and world markets and to reduce expensive imports that state authorities often wanted to discourage.

Families in these areas came to rely on income from both small farm plots and handicraft work; family members worked longer hours and throughout the year to survive. Growth in the commercial agricultural and industrial sectors brought new wealth to some that was visible in such products as cotton dresses. Even the poor were buying more; in one weaving village in Württemberg, for example, girls from relatively poor weaving households were bringing the occasional silk item along with their dowries by the end of the eighteenth century.[18]

But these changes brought new tensions as well, often manifested in generational conflicts. The labor that these new industries required could be provided by peasant sons and daughters needing a portion to marry. The very availability of income outside of the traditional peasant household economy seems, in some regions at least, to have loosened family and community oversight of sexuality and marriage and broken the links between land inheritance and marriage. Rates of illegitimacy skyrocketed in many regions of Europe toward the end of the eighteenth century. Even though some peasants, artisans, and putting-out workers prospered during the economic expansion that peaked in the late eighteenth century, the unevenly distributed social costs of economic growth were manifested in increased workloads, especially for women, and rising rates of infant mortality, illegitimacy, divorce, and poverty. Even for those couples who might expect to eventually inherit a farm, the period of waiting could be long and uncertain.

What younger generations were doing, in effect, was waiting around for the older generation to disappear through death or retirement. As farmland became scarcer with population growth and impoverishment in many regions of Europe apparent by the mid-eighteenth century, there is evidence of a new degree of impatience, anger, or despair, as young people saw little hope of inheritance. This impatience manifested itself, for example, in an Austrian folksong dating from the early nineteenth century entitled "Voda, wann gibst ma denn's Hoamatl" (or, "Father, when ya gonna gimme the farm"):

Father, when ya gonna gimme the farm,
Father, when ya gonna sign it away?
My girl's been growin' every day,
And single no longer wants to stay.

Father, when ya gonna gimme the farm,
Father, when ya gonna gimme the house,
When ya gonna retire to your room out of the way,
And dig up your potatoes all day?[19]

The close connections between family and farming, for all of the tensions, survived through the late eighteenth century or even longer throughout much of Western and Central Europe. If on slave plantations people had to struggle to hold on to tenuous and vulnerable family ties, on peasant farms in Europe there was no escaping family. These changing family connections were part of a larger transformation as local agricultural economies entered more fully into global market networks.

CHAPTER 6

Families in Revolutionary Times (1750–1920)

Anna Altmann's wistful comparison of her 1850s childhood in Bohemia, in Central Europe, with what she imagined childhood to be like among the upper classes draws a direct connection between family life and social class divisions in the context of Europe's Industrial Revolution:

> The garlands woven by the proletariat on the path through life aren't like those of the rich and fortunate, because by the cradle of the proletarian child there stand behind the actual parents a second couple—Father Sorrow and Mother Need—who also claim their rights. When I recall today, now past the noon of life, images from the past, the first to emerge are the dark shadows of my ruined youth. The golden days that the children of the rich enjoyed under the protection of their guardians were never granted to me or to hundreds of others. My sixth birthday had barely passed when I had to enter the factory, to earn a share of my keep.[1]

Altmann's memoir captures the class-specific consequences the economic transformations of the era of industrialization brought to working-class and wealthy families. Diverging experiences of childhood were among the most visible manifestations of this class difference. Politicized workers like Altmann used their personal stories of deprived childhoods as cultural weapons of class warfare.

Although we associate industrialization with modern factories, the transformation of the European economy actually began with rural "protoindustry"—that is, production of goods like cloth, beads, or toys through handicraft work in homes and small shops that came before the factory. By around 1800, families in many rural areas of Europe were making a living by combining farming small plots of land with producing manufactured goods for merchants who sold them on regional or even global mass markets.

This type of industrial production played a large role in the eventual development of Europe's factory industry, and changing patterns of family labor are at the heart of the story. The example of the cotton industry is especially important. Cotton goods had been produced by handicraft means in India, China, Africa, and the New World for many centuries. They entered Europe in appreciable amounts beginning in the seventeenth century as part of the new colonial trade. Some English entrepreneurs decided that it would make economic sense to create a domestic cotton industry rather than importing ever greater quantities of cotton from India. Establishing a domestic cotton manufacturing industry required the importation of raw cotton fiber, which in turn fueled the establishment of slave plantations in European colonies; the import of manufactured cotton cloth from India to England was banned to cut off Indian competition with domestic cloth.

Entrepreneurs involved in developing the manufacture of cotton cloth in England wanted to find ways to lower production costs, and they focused their attention on labor productivity. In 1733, Joseph Kay's invention of the flying shuttle sped up weaving on the hand-operated looms that weavers used. Weavers could now weave cloth much faster than before, but yarn shortages prevented increased production. Much cloth production was still done in small shops and homes in a family labor system. Often, men wove and women and children spun. But the flying shuttle disrupted the balance, since the spinners in a household or region could not spin yarn fast enough to keep up with the weavers.

Textile merchants and entrepreneurs responded by looking for ways to speed up the spinning process and by reorganizing production so that the two processes were separate and more firmly under their control, rather than under the control of the weavers' households. By 1770, spinners were using a new spinning machine, the spinning jenny, which allowed a single spinster to spin thread onto many spools at once.

The need for and success of machines like the spinning jenny thus had as much to do with family labor patterns as with technological advances. The jenny (as its name suggests) was designed for machine operators imagined to be young women, the segment of the labor force that had traditionally spun yarn by hand to supply mostly male home weavers. The shape and design of the original jenny fitted it for use by a young female worker; larger or older workers found it uncomfortable. Similarly, the calico printing processes whereby brightly colored designs were imprinted on cotton cloth also were designed for a female or child labor force with relatively small and dexterous fingers.[2]

Because spinning was the first fully mechanized industry in Europe, the young women and children who predominated in spinning became the world's first modern factory labor force. In the large cotton spinnery established near Waterford on the south coast of Ireland in 1835, for example, 42 percent of the mill's employees were girls under the age of twenty-one.[3]

This pattern prevailed in many of the modern textile mills elsewhere in Europe that took up the British factory model. Jean Bonnet, a self-made man who owned silk mills near Lyon in France, was the model of a modern factory owner. According to Edward Watherston, a British journalist who wrote in the 1870s about Bonnet's factory, Bonnet recruited young girls from the poor agricultural families of the region "under promise to give them board, lodging, clothes, and all that they required, together with small wages, and to teach them not only the art of silk making, but to give them a general education." Bonnet's establishment boasted dormitories staffed by members of religious orders who maintained strict discipline, a useful weapon, according to Watherston, in the struggle "to tame these little savages into order."[4]

The first half of the nineteenth century was an era of diminishing real income and increased working hours for many European families who made their living from the combination of agriculture and industrial work. Since these families survived by pooling the earnings of several family members, a large number of whom had to leave home to find their livelihood, they experienced early industrialization as a family crisis.

Working-class families in factory towns also faced new hardships. They could find work, but employers often preferred women and children, who typically earned less than men, for many types of factory work. Work roles and home life were equally disrupted. This was apparent in working-class family life in Manchester, one of early industrial England's boom towns, as viewed in the 1840s by Friedrich Engels. Engels, who later joined forces with Karl Marx to write treatises critical of industrial capitalism and to help found the socialist movement, observed that "in many families the wife, like the husband, has to work away from home, and the consequence is the total neglect of the children, who are either locked up or given out to be taken care of."[5]

In contrast with the working-class industrial slums, the middle-class residential squares and suburbs in and around England's industrial cities reflected a self-conscious reorganization of urban space to create new, class-segregated spaces for middle-class family life. Again, this was apparent to Engels in Manchester, where, he observed, "the upper

The workforce at a silk spinnery in southern France gathers for a photograph, taken around 1900. Most of the workers are very young girls who were recruited from nearby farms and lived at the factory. Photograph by Claudius Corne. Issued as a postcard entitled "Personnel interne de la Maison C.J. Bonnet, à Jujurieux (Ain)."

bourgeoisie in remoter villas with gardens . . . in free, wholesome country air, in fine, comfortable homes, passed once every half or quarter hour by omnibuses going into the city. And the finest part of the arrangement is this, that the members of this money aristocracy can take the shortest road through the middle of all the labouring districts to their places of business, without ever seeing that they are in the midst of the grimy misery that lurks to the right and the left."[6]

In stark contrast with the working-class mother whose children, social critics feared, lived dangerously in the streets or the mills, mothering in middle-class families took on an unprecedented intensity. To offer but one example, in one northern French industrial region in the late nineteenth century, a certain Madame B. closely supervised the upbringing of her eight children. She kept a notebook about each of them among the family's records. Aiming to "purge them of all evil thoughts and actions," she grilled them frequently to keep herself informed about their thoughts, and withheld goodnight kisses when they misbehaved.[7]

Even though middle-class families exalted the privacy and seclusion of their refuges from the harsh world of the industrial city, images of idealized families reached workers through the circulation of images and stories, through their own observations as domestic servants in upper-class homes, and even in store window displays of children's toys.

Contrasts between, for example, the care devoted to upper-class children and the hard work that was often the fate of working-class children fueled class resentments apparent in workers' memoirs of the era of industrialization. Julius Bruhns, for example, who was born in 1860 in the Hamburg suburb of Altona, recalled in his memoir his feelings as a young child working—in this case in the cigar shop where he began to work at age five:

> My mother's heart bled when she saw her dear little one so tormented, but what was she to do? So I had to spend the largest part of my "golden youth" in the dusty, smoky room of the cigar manufactory, always living and working among adults, while my more fortunate age mates ran around in the bright sunshine in the streets.[8]

The era of the Industrial Revolution in Europe was also punctuated by political revolutions, beginning with the French Revolution of 1789. Because Europe's monarchs had based their claims to power on dynastic principles—that is, the right to rule was based on inheritance of the throne through family lines—rebellion against monarchs also called family ties into question. Family relationships were linked explicitly to the revolutionary process in many different ways.

At the level of political theory and symbolism, overthrowing a king also challenged the rule of the father. A sustained attack on kingly authority had been an important element of a broader Enlightenment-era questioning of social and political institutions. In the private salons and public cafes that multiplied in Europe's cities in the eighteenth century, as well as in the newspapers and magazines that circulated in increasing numbers, thinkers and writers who presented themselves as citizens of the international "republic of letters" applied scientific discoveries and philosophic ideas to problems of everyday life. The new ideas often challenged or sidestepped religious authority; Enlightenment authors looked for new models for human social and political relations. Instead of basing arguments on Scripture (as Luther, for example, had done during the Protestant Reformation) they turned to "Nature," and "Nature's laws." Prominent among the many social and political institutions that were subject to scrutiny and discussion during the Enlightenment era were the political system of absolute monarchy and the patriarchal family. Surprisingly often these two arenas were linked together in the thinking of prominent Enlightenment political theorists.

The Baron de Montesquieu, for example, published a treatise entitled *The Spirit of the Laws* (1752). He used comparative analyses of different regimes to criticize royal despotism in France as well as its justification through analogies with the father's domination of the family. Montesquieu argued against the view that kingly authority was justifiable as a reflection of the "natural" power of the father. According to Montesquieu:

> Some think that nature having established paternal authority, the most natural government was that of a single person. *But the example of paternal authority proves nothing.* For if the power of a father relates to a single government, that of brothers after the death of a father, and that of cousins-german [that is, first cousins] after the decease of brothers, refer to a government of many.
>
> Better is it to say, that the government most conformable to nature is that which best agrees with the humour and disposition of the people in whose favour it is established.[9]

Other Enlightenment political theorists looked to the domestic realm—the realm of the family—for inspiration in their search for a new human order. The two realms were explicitly gendered, the public realm as masculine and the domestic realm as feminine. New kinds of representations of women as virtuous heroines and self-sacrificing mothers and of family life as a realm of personal fulfillment began to circulate in text and image. Women, especially in their role as mother, began to appear in novels and treatises as the guarantors of individual and collective progress through their moral influence on their children.

The French Enlightenment philosopher Jean-Jacques Rousseau presented his ideas about women and family life in different genres. He wrote influential treatises on political theory such as *The Social Contract*, which attacked despotic monarchy as a violation of "natural law," and also popular fictional works such as *Emile*, which exalted simple domestic virtue as more "natural" than the corrupt aristocratic lifestyle of royal court and capital cities. Rousseau proposed a stark and complementary contrast between the feminine domestic sphere and the masculine world of public life:

> Men and women are made for each other, but their mutual dependence differs in degree . . . he could do without her better than she can do without him. She cannot fulfil her purpose in life without his aid, without his goodwill, without his respect . . . Nature herself has decreed that woman, both for herself and her children, should be at the mercy of man's judgment . . .
>
> Once it is demonstrated that men and women neither are nor [should be], constituted the same . . . it follows that they should not have the same education . . . Boys want movement and noise, drums, tops, toy-carts; girls prefer things which appeal to the eye, and can be

Paintings like this 1830 watercolor by Friedrich Wilhelm Doppelmayr, depicting a middle-class family in their home, were produced in increasing numbers toward the beginning of the nineteenth century. Middle-class families commissioned these paintings to record their homes and lifestyles and to preserve family images for posterity. bpk, Berlin / Germanisches Nationalmuseum / Photo: Lutz Braun / Art Resource, NY

used for dressing-up . . . The doll is the girl's special plaything; this shows her instinctive bent towards her life's work. Little girls always dislike learning to read and write, but they are always ready to learn to sew . . . The search for abstract and speculative truths for principles and axioms in science, for all that tends to wide generalizations, is beyond a woman's grasp.[10]

Many women readers—and he had thousands of female fans—loved Rousseau because he infused mothering and the domestic work ascribed to women with moral weight and significance, even if he at the same time limited women to the home. Rousseau's presumption that women's place was "naturally" in the home brought deep contradictions into emerging Enlightenment ideas about citizenship. These ideas would come to the fore during the French Revolution, but the critiques linking family power and political rule were clearly debated before the outbreak of the revolt in 1789.

The effort to reform tyrannical rule by the French king that began in 1789 soon turned into outright rejection of monarchy. King Louis XVI and his queen Marie Antoinette were executed in 1792, and France was declared a republic—that is, a state ruled by representatives of the French people rather than by a royal family. Other European dynasties would eventually form a military alliance against the French republic, and there was continuous warfare between France and the rest of Europe until the restoration of monarchial rule in 1815.

During the period between 1789 and 1815, both family and political relationships were the focus of questions and debates in France and beyond.[11] With the abolition of kingship based on patriarchal principles, how was political authority to be justified? What did overthrowing the king mean for the paternal authority in the family? For gender and generational relations? The revolutionary principles of liberty, equality, and fraternity suggested that more egalitarian relationships—those of brotherhood—were to replace the unequal relationship between father and sons inherent in monarchy. But what about sisters and wives?

New and often conflicting definitions of citizenship were quick to emerge. In 1791, a Constitutional Assembly was elected by active citizens—defined as men whose annual taxes equaled the local wages paid for three days of labor. This was a huge extension of the politically empowered population, but it still disenfranchised half of the adult men and all the women of France. Slavery was abolished in France and the French Empire in 1791, but freed slaves were not given full civil rights either. These groups—poor men, women, former slaves—did nevertheless claim rights by participating in political demonstrations, political clubs, and militias, and even through their manner of dressing, for example by adopting red "liberty caps" that signified support for the Revolution.

The overthrow of the royal father signaled domestic as well as public rebellion. An actress named Olympe de Gouges had the audacity to rewrite the Revolution's key manifesto, "The Declaration of Rights of Man and Citizen," to include women. For its statement "Men are born and remain free and equal in rights," she substituted "Woman is born free and remains equal to man in rights."[12]

Mary Wollstonecraft, a British woman inspired by the Revolution, went to Paris to witness events there for herself. In 1792, she published a treatise, *A Vindication of the Rights of Woman*, that demonstrates how the Revolution offered an opportunity to turn Enlightenment ideals about gender and family politics in a more radical direction. Addressing the ideas of Rousseau directly, Wollstonecraft offered a different view of gender and politics:

What opinion are we to form of a system of education, when the author [that is, Rousseau, in *Emile*] says . . . 'Educate women like men, and the more they resemble our sex the less power will they have over us.' This is the very point I am at. I do not wish them to have power over men, but over themselves . . . make women rational creatures, and free citizens, and they will quickly become good wives, and mothers.[13]

Despite the arguments of writers like de Gouges and Wollstonecraft, women were never granted citizenship rights by the revolutionary assemblies, but family laws were reformed in ways that did much to address family inequalities and women's complaints about domestic tyranny. All sons and daughters were given equal rights to inheritance. Distinctions between the rights of legitimate and illegitimate children were eliminated. Marriage became a civil contract rather than a religious covenant, and divorce was made possible on a variety of grounds and at the demand of wives as well as husbands. Far more women than men took advantage of the new laws to extricate themselves from untenable, even abusive, relationships, suggesting that for all of the limitations in the public realm, the revolution did at least temporarily bring transformation to the domestic realm.[14]

If the early phases of the revolution linked the overthrow of monarchy with a new family order, its later phases and its eventual defeat brought a backlash against the democratization of the family that had to some extent paralleled efforts to democratize political life. This reversion was perhaps best expressed in law and in symbol in the regime of Napoleon, who came to power as a result of the revolution but who would take it in a new direction. In the course of the 1790s, the fragile First Republic of France fell apart. Its leadership increasingly alienated itself from its own supporters through its repression of political opposition at home. The government relied on conquest abroad to sustain its popularity and its finances. It was a short step from a civilian government dependent on military successes for its popularity to military dictatorship, which arrived with Napoleon's coup d'état in 1799.

The French Revolution ended, for all intents and purposes, with Napoleon's takeover. Many of the reforms of the early years were undone. Napoleon would eventually declare himself emperor, in political and symbolic terms bringing back the rule of the father. He did codify law for the French Empire, which meant that his rule was constitutional and not arbitrary. However, he undid important revolutionary reforms, most notably in the realm of marriage and divorce. In post-Napoleonic France, wives could not act in a legal capacity independently of their husbands; the authority of fathers over children was also increased. The Napoleonic law code introduced explicit inequalities between wives and husbands in divorce law. A man could sue his wife for divorce on grounds of adultery, but a wife could sue her husband on these grounds only if he actually brought his mistress into the family home. Nevertheless, even with the reversals of many of the more egalitarian impulses of the early Revolution, the memory of overthrow of monarchy would serve as a model for later antimonarchical insurrections in Europe and beyond. And for all its complexities, the universal claims to human rights that the Revolution introduced would continue to be called upon as grounds for rethinking both public and domestic tyranny.

Europe's "dual revolutions"—industrial and political—involved profound changes in the family. Elsewhere in the world, industrialization and political upheavals in the modern era took different forms, but they too held implications for family life. The fact that industrialization happened first in England and Europe made a difference in its history in the rest of the world.

Chinese modern industrialization came in the wake of European imperialist ventures in the second half of the nineteenth century. A series of defeats by Western powers of the Chinese Empire under the rule of the Qing dynasty, beginning with the Opium War in 1840, resulted in treaties that granted foreigners economic and political rights in China. By the end of the nineteenth century, Chinese intellectuals and officials had become convinced of the need to adopt modern science and industrial technologies in order to compete with Western powers, but they debated how best to achieve this without losing what they termed China's "essence."

Their efforts led to the so-called Hundred Days of Reform in 1898. The Qing Emperor Guangxu, who ruled from 1875 to 1908, had called for proposals to reform the government. Reformers proposed changes in the educational system, substantial investment in industry and the military, and the establishment of a constitutional monarchy. The latter proposal in particular went farther than the young emperor and the empress dowager Cixi were willing to go. (Cixi was the emperor's aunt and also his adoptive mother; she played an important behind-the-scenes role in imperial politics from 1861 until her death in 1908.) Several of the key figures in the reform were arrested and executed, and the only durable result of the reform was the establishment of Peking University. It became clear after the failure of these reform efforts that the capacity of the imperial government and the ruling dynasty to reform itself was limited.

Revolutionary ideas, both in China and among Chinese living abroad, began to spread. There were many charges made against the Qing dynasty, but one of them was that they were not "Chinese" and therefore had put the interests of the dynasty ahead of the interests of the Chinese nation. (The Qing ruling family were Manchus, descended from seminomadic northern peoples from Manchuria, who had conquered China in 1644.) In a tract called *The Revolutionary Army* (1903), the young revolutionary activist Zou Rong identified the problem facing China in terms that are explicitly racial:

> Internally we are the slaves of the Manchus and suffering from their tyranny and externally we are being harassed by the [western] Powers, and we are doubly enslaved. The reason why our sacred Han race, descendants of the Yellow Emperor, should support revolutionary independence arises precisely from the question of whether our race will go under and be exterminated.[15]

Zou Rong died in jail two years after writing the tract, which had enormous influence in promoting a new kind of nationalism, fueled both by opposition to foreign imperialism and by opposition to the Qing dynasty, widely perceived as foreign. Zou Rong suggests that the Han Chinese people, those from the empire's traditional homeland, bear a family and blood affinity because of their descent from a single mythical ancestor. This blood affinity was important in the construction of Chinese nationalism in the early part of the twentieth century.

The first decade of the twentieth century saw a number of unsuccessful revolts against the Qing dynasty; in 1911, after what seemed to be just another uprising in Wuhan, the army mutinied and the dynasty was actually overthrown. No one, not even the army, was willing to fight to preserve the dynasty. The revolutionary forces had been unified in their opposition to the Manchu rulers. However, after the fall of the dynasty they were deeply divided about what path China should take. The resulting civil wars lasted until mainland China was once again unified under Communist rule in 1949. Throughout this revolutionary era, the family was central to discussions about China's future. Some observers regarded the family as a site for the preservation of what was good about the Chinese past; many revolutionaries, in contrast, rooted China's problems in family relations that would need to be transformed to prepare China for a modern future.

That future included both political and economic modernization. Modern industrial factories, which first appeared in the early twentieth century, brought women workers out of the household in unprecedented numbers. When modern factories first appeared in the early twentieth century, they typically recruited young women workers from the countryside. As in Europe, young women were seen as ideal textile workers because of their presumed manual dexterity and docility. In some regions, labor recruiters went out in the countryside and brought back girls, who typically ranged in age from fourteen to eighteen, to work in factories. The recruiters paid the girls' families a lump sum for their daughters' labor.

Sometimes girls lived with the families of the recruiters, but more often they lived in dormitories, where their comings and goings (and their virtue) were closely guarded. Since their pay was normally sent back to their families in the countryside, it was in the interests of their families to delay their daughters' marriages, because a married woman would typically stop working in the mills; if she did continue working, her paycheck would no longer go to her birth family but rather to her husband's family. Still, most of the young women did eventually marry, and their marriages were almost always arranged by their parents as they had been in the past. The factory pattern that encouraged female workers' geographic mobility was certainly a new factor in Chinese family life. But it did not radically transform family life; daughters' earnings still went into the family budget, and parents still controlled marriage choices. Indeed, many women factory workers regarded free choice of marriage partners (something that political reformers at the time were advocating) as rather scandalous.[16] Yang Meizhen, a sociology student who conducted interviews with women workers in the late 1920s, reported that the young women "think that the idea of free marriages, men and women engaging marriages by themselves, is disgraceful."[17]

At the same time that poor rural girls were providing the labor in modernizing Chinese cities, especially Shanghai, reformers and business people in Shanghai and elsewhere in China were discussing the ways in which the emergent Chinese middle class should be reformed to best position China for a new role in the modern world. The ideal Chinese household in the past had been multigenerational; wealthy men often kept concubines in addition to a wife. However, in the eyes of reformers in the early twentieth century, this older family system was precisely the problem, the source of China's shortcomings in comparison with the West. Senior generations dominated the young, and men dominated women. Patriarchal customs and concubinage came under attack by reformers who regarded these practices as outmoded vestiges of a corrupt era.

The May Fourth Movement, so called because it began with protests on May 4, 1919, over the terms of the Treaty of Versailles, brought questions of family and politics to the fore. The movement began at Peking University among students and spread to include students and workers in other cities. The May Fourth Movement's analysis of Chinese society identified Confucianism, especially as it was manifested in strict family and social hierarchies, as the root of China's problems.

Chen Duxiu, one of the leaders of the movement and also one of the founders of the Chinese Communist Party, described the ways in which Confucian teachings about the family had inhibited the growth of modern political consciousness: "When people are bound by the Confucian teachings of filial piety and obedience to the point of the son not deviating from the father's way even three years after his death and the woman obeying not only her husband and her father but her son, how can they form their own political party and make their own choice?"[18] The liberation of the young and the emancipation of women were key elements of the program of the movement. The May Fourth Movement also advocated the promotion of science and democracy in China. The prominence of young people (many of the leaders were students), including many young women, symbolized the overthrow of patriarchal authority both at home and in the political arena.

Amid general cries for the overthrow of the old family system, specific plans for new-style families were put forth by both businessmen and political reformers. You Huaigao, an entrepreneurial dairy farmer, published a magazine called *Family Weekly* (1936) that was at least in part designed to increase demand for milk products. He argued that the "small family," by which he meant the Western nuclear family, was "the family form suitable to the new age."[19] In You's vision, modern families were formed by partners who chose one another and were monogamous. They consumed modern commercial products and participated in the commercial economy as consumers. Such families were portrayed in the popular press as politically progressive and economically efficient. Journals were full of advertisements for products such as soap and medicine that would assist Chinese families in their efforts to live modern lives. Journals published photographs of modern living spaces that made visible the connection between modernity and western styles.

But the very fact that the new small family could be regarded as an imitation of the Western family led to concern and countercriticism. The influx of Western goods and ideas aroused an anti-Western opposition that found expression in movements that encouraged Chinese

玲瓏圖畫雜誌　第一卷　第一期

現代家庭陳設應有之改革

（梁雪清）

編輯雜誌　畫圖文華　丹青爲精　女士梁雪清

就各時代之人物藝術思想而論，我們膽量將秦漢、唐宋、夏商周之老祖宗所產生之藝術推翻，又難道我們不能創作生代之新藝術？舊式家庭陳設，陰深泥古，沉悶之途徑，嚴肅蕭靜，古雅，避高應沉，思想沉悼，呆板活潑之設置，縱求嚴肅，最新，……我們在前領導，再念許多一般呆板之室裝飾，吾甚愛之。低限度亦不容我，來約束我們之觀念，生活不能在前，清新簡潔，一洗此室沉鬱陰森之氣，……

▲現代家庭之陳設▼

This article from the first issue of Linglong, *a women's magazine published in Shanghai in 1931, is entitled "The arrangement of a modern household." The article talks about the ways in which it is important for modern people to live in modern surroundings; the photograph illustrates one such modern room with Western-style furnishings of contemporary design.* Linglong *Vol.1, No. 1, 1931, p. 14. Columbia University Libraries*

people to buy local products. The local products movements were connected to a new kind of consumer nationalism also directed toward family purchases.

Enthusiasm for local products extended even to toys—or perhaps especially to toys, since toys were important to children, the future of the nation. In a scene set in the early 1920s, the popular movie *Xiao wanyi* (Little Playthings, 1933) makes clear the relationship between politics, consumption, social class, and urban-rural relations. The female protagonist, who makes old-fashioned handmade toys, says: "These foreign toys are all machine-made in big factories and produced very quickly. The rich children of the city all play with these warships and airplanes. But should we be dejected? No! We will pull ourselves up from the pits of our stomachs and face forward." Later in the film, the same person wonders if city children brought up on foreign toys will ever fight foreigners, clearly expressing concern about the kind of politics children might learn at home.[20]

All sides in the civil war and revolution saw the family and domestic life as the fulcrum of change, the space where the future was emerging, whether or not change was welcome. The "dual revolutions"—economic and political—meant very different things in the world's varied regions. But they were tied everywhere to family transformations.

CHAPTER 7

Powers of Life and Death:
Families in the Era of State Population Management (1880 to the Present)

In 1935, a German woman, Mathilde M., a farmer and mother of seven, was brought before a sterilization board at the suggestion of her doctor, who claimed she was "feeble-minded." The Nazi regime had set up these boards to enforce a new law they passed in 1934, the Law for the Prevention of Offspring with Hereditary Diseases. This law stipulated: "Anyone who is suffering from a hereditary disease can be sterilized by a surgical operation if, according to the experiences of medical science, it is to be expected with great probability that his offspring will suffer from serious hereditary physical or mental defects." Mathilde's doctor had decided that she ought to be sterilized according to this law.[1]

In opposing this recommendation before the board, Mathilde admitted that she did not want more children, but she resisted the state's intervention into her family life and she disputed the claim that she was mentally deficient: "Of course I cannot answer a question about calculating interest, which ninety of one hundred women could not have answered . . . During the day, I have no hours to read or the like, since with the children and 30 acres of land, as well as the animals, I work from morning until late night without rest."[2] Mathilde actually was successful in making her case and so she wasn't sterilized, but others were not so fortunate. Between the passage of the law in 1934 and the end of the Nazi regime in 1945, about 360,000 German men and women were sterilized. They were targets of an especially extreme and vicious state policy designed to manage the population, but the idea that the state had the right and responsibility to implement family policies was hardly new.[3]

European state builders had already begun to think of the inhabitants of their realms, for some purposes, as "populations" as early as the seventeenth century. Population growth and reproduction became the focus of state policy; governments throughout Europe had by the nineteenth century introduced techniques like the household register and census to track population trends. Political theorists and historians see these developments as the beginning of "biopolitics"—that is, routine state surveillance, measurement, and management of human life. By the end of the twentieth century, monitoring and managing populations had become markers of modern states throughout the world.

Families everywhere are shaped by a wide range of state policies, including marriage laws, tax incentives, social security and other welfare programs, laws regulating contraception, support for child care and education, and laws about gender or race relations. Along more sinister lines, some modern states have enacted brutal and even genocidal policies, such as the Nazi sterilization law, aimed at eliminating populations deemed undesirable or unfit.

Many modern welfare states' programs have their roots in late-nineteenth-century initiatives. Sometimes these initiatives came from on high. For example, in 1883 German Chancellor Otto von Bismarck proposed mandatory health insurance for workers, a program that was popular given the level of sickness and injury among workers, but one also designed for political reasons—to lure workers away from the socialist opposition. Some efforts to get the government involved in welfare programs came from below. For example, many British working-class women wrote letters in 1913 and 1914 in support of the Women's Cooperative Guild's campaign for national grants in support of poor mothers. The letters the Guild received recounted tale after tale of the suffering that poor women experienced as the result of too many pregnancies and too little income for food and medical care. One letter writer (the names of the authors were not published by the Guild) recounted how she had nearly died when giving birth to her first child; her doctor had told her she "had worked too hard and not rested sufficiently." Arguing that "the child is the asset of the nation and the mother its backbone," she called for a maternity benefit, a payment that would go to poor mothers at the birth of a child to help her feed and care for the child and herself.[4]

European governments regulated population matters in their colonies as well as at home. Part of the motivation for founding colonies in the first place was to provide spaces where "surplus" European populations could relocate—where the unemployed might find work, unmarried women might find husbands, and the landless might find land. Cecil Rhodes, an advocate of British imperialist expansion, argued in the 1890s that colonies were the key to solving Britain's domestic social conflicts; "in order to save the 40,000,000 inhabitants of the United Kingdom from a bloody civil war, we colonial statesmen must acquire new lands to settle the surplus population, to provide new markets for the goods produced by them."[5] Settlers migrated or in some cases were deported from Great Britain, France, Germany, and elsewhere in Europe to European settler colonies in Africa, South and Southeast Asia, the Americas, and Australia. Population management and family policy in the colonies were linked to population management in European homelands.

Colonial administrators used family metaphors to justify their colonial rule. They treated colonial subjects like children who needed education and enlightened guidance in order to progress to maturity and autonomy; maturity, once accomplished, could bring civic adulthood. For example, African subjects living in French colonies who learned to speak French and who obeyed French laws "could be included in the French family of citizens with a full complement of rights—regardless of skin color." Europeans also drew on their notions about gender relations as a kind of yardstick of civilization; for example, the French justified their "civilizing mission" in Algeria on the claims that women's apparent subservience to men in Islamic culture marked Algeria's cultural backwardness, what one colonial writer termed "the moral malady of Islam." Since French women were not legal equals with men (being denied the vote, among other things, until 1945), this claim was contradictory and even hypocritical.[6]

Actual family, sexual, and gender relations in the colonies shaped colonial rule. In early years of colonial settlement, European men often established sexual liaisons with indigenous women. Some expressed a preference for non-European sexual partners. In the early years of French rule in West Africa, for example, many administrators took local women as concubines; one praised them because "they did not demand constant attention 'like their white sisters.'"[7] But such informal unions became less tenable as European powers sought to establish tighter political authority in their colonies toward the end of the nineteenth century and the beginning of the twentieth. European administrators started to bring their wives and families along, and reproducing European-style domestic life in colonial capitals came to be a central part of the process of the imposition of European civilization.

In German Southwest Africa (now Namibia), marriage and other forms of sexual unions led to complicated disputes among Germans at home, settlers, and colonial administrators between the 1890s and the beginning of World War I in 1914. As in other colonies, some early male settlers had established unions with African women; few of these were legal marriages. Colonial authorities and many settlers feared the prospect of children from such unions demanding German citizenship or inheritance rights; many Germans were opposed on principle to the idea of race mixing in any form (although the concept of race had as yet been nowhere officially defined). Colonial Settlement Commissioner Paul Rohrbach warned in 1904 of the dangers of racial mixture: "every sentiment for morality, culture, social order, and national well-being is lost. The people 'go native' [*verkaffern*], as one says here . . . [the men] sink into a swarm of wild, ill-bred, dirty bastard children. As experience has shown and because of the lack of white girls, many young men are inclined to enter into marital relations with natives, especially Bastard girls."[8]

Political pressure mounted in Germany to encourage the migration of unmarried German women to the colonies, women who would marry the German men there, presumably solving the "problem" of race mixing. Not everyone agreed with this logic, since in many colonies European men continued to establish common-law relationships with indigenous women even where marriages with European women were frequent. The critical economist Moritz Bonn made himself unpopular with German colonial authorities when he claimed in the first decade of the twentieth century that "[t]he main cause of bastardization in Africa was not the absence of white women but the presence of black ones."[9]

Still, the schemes to send unmarried German women as potential wives continued to unfold. The German Colonial Society began by sending two German women to Southwest Africa in 1897, followed by a growing number in later years. Conservative men in the colony, such as the colonial governor Theodor Leutwein, emphasized the need for white women to establish racially pure families.[10] Leutwein was seconded by conservative women such as the Baroness Ada von Lilienkron, who believed that the colony "was completely in danger of going to the Boers [settlers of Dutch origin] and the Kaffirs [European term for South Africa's indigenous people] . . . because a growing race of mixed-bloods threatened from the beginning to nip Germandom in the bud."[11] In 1905, the German government prohibited marriages between German settlers and colonial subjects in Southwest Africa. By 1914, German colonial associations had sent around 600 unmarried German women to Southwest Africa. Most of these women did end up marrying German male settlers.[12]

Similar debates appeared in French colonies. In non-settler colonies such as French West Africa, the arrival of wives of colonial administrators in the 1920s signaled the end of the era of informal empire in the household as well as in the government. Old-style relations of concubinage, and occasional legal marriages, between powerful European men and subservient indigenous women were largely replaced by marriages between European men and women and stricter social and racial distinctions between European and indigenous families.[13]

In settler colonies, family problems intensified. In the late nineteenth century, the French sought to attract large numbers of European settlers to their North African colony of Algeria. In order to attract European settlers, the colonial state altered laws affecting property holding and land transfer, which had the effect of increasing European settler control of land in Algeria to nearly five million acres by 1901.[14] Settlers moved in large numbers from France and southern Europe into Algerian cities as well.

Management of the relationships between settlers and indigenous Algerians required the colonial state to involve itself in all aspects of family life, including the laws that governed marriage and parenthood, labor relations between European employers and Algerian workers, sexuality, reproduction, and inheritance. Colonial authorities counted on European women to disseminate French family norms among indigenous women and thus to help win over indigenous women to colonial rule. However, European women were often attracted to the colonies at least in part because they seemed to offer space for emancipating themselves from the restraints of European norms of propriety and expectations about traditional roles for women. Isabelle Eberhardt, for example, left behind European notions of feminine respectability when she left Europe with her mother to move to Algeria in 1897, when she was twenty years old. She immediately adopted male attire—as she put it, "the egalitarian outfit of the Bedouins"—so that she could roam freely through the Arab quarters of the city of Tunis, "which the attire of a staid young European woman would prevent her from entering." By dressing as a Bedouin man, she was crossing both gender and racial divides. The freedom this allowed her led her into a very different relationship to colonial spaces and people than most other settlers and it presented a troubling alternative to the "civilizing mission" and the model of French family life that colonial authorities sought to establish. Instead of trying to make Algerian women more French, Eberhardt tried to become more Algerian.[15]

Citizenship itself was caught up in family relations and family strategies. In principle, the French claimed, membership in the French political community was open to all regardless of background. However, in practice, ethnic or racial or religious categories transmitted through a combination of family affiliation and cultural assimilation created a myriad of different political relationships to the French state. The children of French parents held unambiguous French citizenship rights even if they had been born in the colony. As part of its effort to encourage European immigration even beyond French nationals, in 1889 the French government passed a law that granted French citizenship to the children born in Algeria of non-French European parents who had settled in the colony and assimilated (these families came mostly from Italy, Spain, or Malta). A few categories of indigenous people also were granted the right to French citizenship, and in some (though not all) cases the right to pass it along to their children; these included Algerian Jews who had been naturalized and select Arabs and Berbers deemed "evolved" enough in their cultural behavior and attitudes. All of the latter were required to renounce adherence to Islamic law, including family law, as Islamic law was deemed inimical to French culture.

Family and population considerations were thus part and parcel of colonial rule. European colonies were also early sites of development of explicitly racialist policies. In Algeria and West Africa, some policies entailed defining population categories in racial or ethnic terms or making different rules for European settlers and colonial subjects, rules that were implicitly racially specific. In some colonies, the solidification of racial boundaries contributed to local campaigns of population relocation or even extermination.

The German colonies in Africa are a case in point. Anticolonial rebellions in German East Africa and Southwest Africa between 1904 and 1908 met with brutal repression. Sixty to 80 percent of the Herero people and 40 to 60 percent of the Nama people in Southwest Africa died as a result of German military actions or as a result of forced relocations.[16] These policies produced the first genocide of the twentieth century. Despite conflict among German state authorities in the colony and in Germany over this ruthless strategy, this policy of repression and lethal relocation can be seen as an extreme version of more widespread colonial practices (such as forcing people to wear identity badges or live in segregated settlements), designed to survey and control indigenous populations.

The fascist movements that came to power in the 1920s and 1930s in Italy and Germany deployed population management techniques in new and destructive ways. The term "fascist" refers specifically to the name of the party that ruled Italy from 1922 to 1943—the Partito Nazionale Fascista—under the leadership of Benito Mussolini. It has also been generalized to refer to similar parties elsewhere during the same era. These parties shared a political philosophy that elevated the nation or race above the individual, idealized a strong leader who ruled over a centralized government and embodied the nation, regimented economy and society in the name of the nation, and suppressed opposition.[17] Fascist leaders in Italy and Germany—Mussolini and Adolf Hitler, respectively—thought of the national population as a biological unit, a body that needed to grow and expand or die out. Their regimes emphasized military strength and the economic development necessary for that strength. But also, and importantly, they introduced measures to encourage the right sort of reproduction and to marginalize or eliminate unwanted groups in the population.

Mussolini's definition of fascism made the movement's biological dimensions clear. He wrote: "For Fascism, the growth of empire, that is to say the expansion of the nation, is an essential manifestation of vitality, and its opposite a sign of decadence. Peoples which are rising, or rising again after a period of decadence, are always imperialist; and renunciation [of imperialism] is a sign of decay and of death."[18] From the start, Mussolini emphasized a reinvigorated family as fundamental to his vision. State policy and propaganda emphasized biological differences between men and women and called for sex-specific forms of national affiliation: hypermasculine roles in the military and the industrial workforce for men, and hyperfeminine roles centering on reproduction for women.

The state passed laws taxing bachelors and punishing homosexuals; it encouraged large families; abortion and dissemination of birth control information were made state crimes.[19] The Italian fascist state in some sense substituted for fathers by providing support for mothers in the form of family allowances for their children or health coverage for maternity care, and also symbolically, for example, in a campaign that asked married women to contribute their wedding rings to be melted down to support Mussolini's rearmament campaign.[20] These policies politicized the family and explicitly connected formerly private family decisions with state policy.

In Germany, the exaggerated emphasis on biological and reproductive aspects of state policy was evident from the very beginnings of Nazism. The Party's first program, proclaimed by Hitler in 1920 in Munich, demanded "the unification of all Germans in the Greater Germany on the

This newspaper advertisement for the 1935 Italian fascist campaign encourages women to donate their wedding rings to the national cause of building up the army. Putting the rings into a military helmet dramatizes the fact that women are being encouraged to sacrifice their most prized possession to support the troops. "Le Sanzioni," Domenica del Corriere, *December 18, 1935. Courtesy of the University of Wisconsin Digital Collections Center*

basis of the right of self-determination of peoples" and "land and territory (colonies) for the sustenance of our people, and colonization for our surplus population." The program further specified that "[o]nly a member of the race can be a citizen. A member of the race can only be one who is of German blood, without consideration of creed. Consequently no Jew can be a member of the race."[21] The language of the Party program makes it clear that Jews and Germans were regarded as separate "races."

Nazism differed from Italian fascism in that the role of racial thinking as an explicit element of national belonging was clearer from the start; its specific racialist policies, only fully worked out once the party came to power, were also more intrusive and more coercive. Hitler's deputy Rudolf Hess termed Nazism "applied biology," picking up on a phrase used by the geneticist Fritz Lenz in a prominent text on human heredity published in 1932.[22] Hitler's regime held up the so-called Nordic race as its ideal and attempted to mold Germany into a cohesive national community that excluded anyone deemed racially foreign or biologically unfit. This entailed entering the realm of the family—including decisions about marriage and conception—to an unprecedented extent.

The Nazi regime wanted to increase birthrates among those deemed racially elite. Once the Party seized power in 1933, one of its first measures was the Law for the Encouragement of Marriage. This law stated that newly married couples of Aryan race could get a government loan, a portion of which would be forgiven at the birth of each child. In a 1934 speech, Hitler laid out the central place of reproduction in his political vision: "In my state, the mother is the most important citizen . . . the program of our National Socialist Women's movement has in reality but one single point, and that point is the child, that tiny creature which must be born and grow strong and which alone gives meaning to the whole life-struggle."

In contrast to its encouragement of marriage and reproduction among the Aryan racial elite, the Nazi regime passed measures to prevent reproduction among those deemed inferior. The Nazi government also enacted the Law for the Prevention of Offspring with Hereditary Diseases shortly after taking power in 1933. According to this law:

> Anyone suffering from a hereditary disease can be sterilized by a surgical operation if, according to the experience of medical science, there is a high probability that his offspring will suffer from serious physical or mental defects of a hereditary nature. Anyone suffering from any of the following diseases is considered hereditarily diseased under this law: 1. Congenital mental deficiency, 2. Schizophrenia, 3. Manic-depression, 4. Hereditary epilepsy, 5. Hereditary St. Vitus' Dance (Huntington's Chorea), 6. Hereditary blindness, 7. Hereditary deafness, 8. Serious hereditary physical deformity. Furthermore, anyone suffering from chronic alcoholism can be sterilized.[23]

This law reflected the opinion of those scientists of the time who advocated eugenic policies—that is, programs designed to "improve" the genetic qualities of a population. German medical personnel, lawyers, and scientists cooperated with the law and sat on the boards determining whether or not a person would be sterilized. Most of the early victims of the sterilization policy were, like Mathilde M., poor women categorized as "Aryan"; however, this early eugenic sterilization was a precedent for the explicitly racist sterilization and other medical

An ideal "Aryan" family gathers in this Nazi party poster. The phrase on the poster proclaims that Volksgenossen *(that is, "racial comrades") need help and advice and asks the reader to go to the local Nazi office to volunteer. The image of the needy family and the accompanying appeal for help illustrates the centrality of racial regeneration to the Nazi program.* Hoover Institution Political Poster Database, Stanford University

experiments later undertaken at the concentration camps that imprisoned Jews, homosexuals, and Gypsies—all deemed as racially inferior populations—along with political prisoners.

In addition to sterilization, Germany passed two other laws in 1935 to regulate reproduction. The Marital Health Law banned sexual unions between the "hereditarily healthy" and the "unfit." The Blood Protection Laws, also known as the Nuremberg Laws, criminalized marriage or sexual relations between Jews and non-Jews in particular, although in formulating the law there was discussion over whether other "non-Aryan" races should also be included in the ban.

Fascist population measures were extreme, but the thinking behind them circulated well beyond the borders of Germany. A 1936 Nazi propaganda poster proclaimed: "We are not alone." On the poster, a woman holding a baby is protected by a man holding a shield bearing the title of the 1933 sterilization law. The family is surrounded by the flags of all of the nations of the world which had either already passed or were considering some form of voluntary or coercive sterilization program.[24]

Some American eugenicists applauded Nazi policy and viewed their sterilization program as exemplary. In his 1934 book *The Case for Sterilization*, American eugenicist Leon Whitney wrote: "Many farsighted men and women in both England and America have long been working earnestly toward something very like what Hitler has now made compulsory."[25] In fact, there had been forced sterilization laws passed in several U.S. states as early as 1907. Sterilization gained support as a means of reducing costs for the care of the poor, especially as poverty levels rose during the depression of the 1930s.[26]

Meanwhile, in South Africa, the white supremacist Nationalist party was growing in strength on the platform of establishing a more explicitly racialist regime. The laws it soon passed after coming to power in the 1940s and formally establishing the apartheid regime echoed many of the Nazi policies. The Prohibition of Mixed Marriages Act of 1949 prohibited marriages between white people and people of other races, and the Immorality Amendment Act of 1950 went on to prohibit extramarital sex between white and black people. In the same year, further acts were passed to create a register that would record every South African person's race; subsequent forced removals and relocations aimed to create geographic separation among races as well.

While eugenic science and the depression spurred coercive population measures such as sterilization in some countries, in many European democracies national political responses to the economic crisis more typically emphasized social welfare measures such as public works, subsidies for food or family home mortgages, and increased unemployment benefits. (These types of programs also were introduced in the United States under the New Deal.) But whether in the benign and popular form of welfare state measures aimed at healthier babies or the sinister form of fascist racial policies, biopolitical thinking informed state policies across and beyond Europe by the mid-twentieth century; thereafter, family and politics would never be far apart.

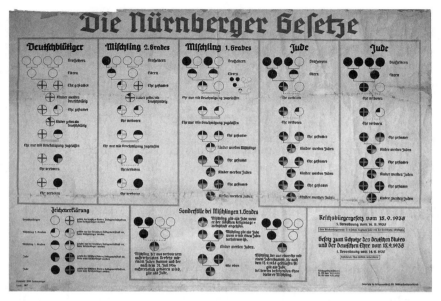

This chart summarizes the Nuremberg Laws, which the Nazi government passed in 1935 to restrict marriages between Jews and "Aryans." These laws required evidence from family genealogy for permission to marry. People with four German grandparents (white circles) were categorized as of "German blood"; others were categorized as "Jewish" or "Mixed" depending on the number of grandparents in each category. The chart spells out which types of marital unions were allowed and which prohibited. United States Holocaust Memorial Museum, N13862. The view or opinions expressed in this book and the context in which the images are used do not necessarily reflect the views or policy of, nor imply approval by or endorsement by, the United States Holocaust Memorial Museum.

World War II, like virtually all wars, brought serious changes in family life in the combatant nations. Families were broken up by the departure of troops and military fatalities, and also by massive civilian casualties and dislocations during and after the war. On the home front, workforce mobilizations brought new workers into factories that supplied the war effort. For example, the huge influx of women into the industrial work force in the United States changed family dynamics even as it helped to mobilize the country for the war effort. As symbolized by Rosie the Riveter, this wartime recruitment increased the number of working American women by over 40 percent between 1940 and 1944. Although many of these women would leave the workforce after the war, levels of women's participation in work outside the home would never again descend to prewar levels.[27]

The war's end brought a breakdown of the coalition of antifascist Allied Powers, which had included both the United States and the Soviet

Union. By the late 1940s, these two world powers had ceased their war-time cooperation and had taken on leadership positions in two hostile camps vying for global domination. The family was an important site of confrontation in the Cold War between the U.S.-led capitalist West and the Soviet-led communist East between 1945 and 1990.

The idealized U.S. family of the 1950s and early 1960s was both a site of escape from the political anxieties of war and the Cold War "Atomic Age" and an ideological demonstration of the superiority of the American way of life. Couples rushed to marry and start families after the war. A higher proportion of Americans got married than ever before or since, and they married younger. The number of children they bore also increased during this era, even though contraception was widely available for the first time, especially after the approval of the birth control pill in 1960.[28]

Federally funded mortgages fuelled the purchase of an unprecedented number of single-family homes, which in turn encouraged the development of new suburban lifestyles and the consumption of modern furniture and household appliances. The GI Bill's provision of free college and trade school educations for (mostly male) veterans, in the form of tuition paid directly to the GI's school of choice, and subsidies for home purchases reinforced the model of the male breadwinner by preparing men for careers, even as some married women remained in the paid workforce.

In the Soviet Union and its satellite states in Eastern Europe, the emphasis was on creating institutional support to allow women to combine paid work and childrearing. In one famous confrontation between the two powers, the so-called Kitchen Debate that took place at an exposition of American products in Moscow in 1959, family lifestyle was at the center. The Soviet premier Nikita Khrushchev criticized American families for their inequalities and their trivialization of women. U.S. vice president Richard Nixon touted American women's reliance on modern appliances as a sign of their superior status under capitalism. This confrontation dramatized the juxtaposition of the capitalist and communist ideals of the family, but beneath the rhetoric, real historical changes demonstrate the particularly close links between family and politics in the Cold War era.

After the defeat of Germany in 1945, the Allied Powers divided the country among themselves for a period of military occupation and administration. The Soviet-occupied zone eventually established a more permanent identity as the German Democratic Republic (East Germany), and the sectors occupied by the United States, Great Britain, and France became the Federal Republic of Germany (West Germany). The split juxtaposed two types of economy—state socialism in the East and capitalism in the West—and also two types of political regime, the single-party state of the East and the multiparty electoral democracy of the West. But it also juxtaposed two distinctive zones in terms of family policy.

In West Germany, the prevailing norm was the male breadwinner with a home-oriented wife—a traditional ideal that also represented a continuity with the family glorified by Nazism. Although the number of women working outside the home in West Germany was, as elsewhere, on the rise by the 1960s, conservative West German family policies meant that these numbers were far lower than elsewhere in Europe. One such policy, a law not repealed until 1977, specified that a married woman had a right to work "only insofar as [is] compatible with her duties within the marriage and the family."[29]

In East Germany, by contrast, communist work and gender norms prevailed. Work was considered central to individual and collective development. Women as well as men were expected to work outside the home, although, as in the U.S.S.R. and elsewhere in Eastern Europe, men were not expected to share in housework. But the government did take measures to support the combination of women's work and mothering.

Beginning in the 1960s, working mothers in East Germany were given eighteen weeks off plus a month's pay at each birth and easier access to housing and loans. In 1976, paid maternity leave was extended to twenty-six weeks, and then eventually to a full year. The workweek for mothers of two children was reduced by three hours per week. The state provided child care; in 1989, more than 70 percent of children under the age of three had state-provided child care, as contrasted with just 5 percent in West Germany. Overall in East Germany, 92 percent of women aged twenty-five to sixty were employed in 1989, whereas the equivalent proportion in the West was 54 percent.

Childrearing was not as strong a disincentive to work outside the home in East Germany as it was in West Germany. In the late 1980s, 20 percent of West German women with one child under age eighteen worked outside the home, while 75 percent of East German women with one child worked outside the home. Figures for women with more than one child reveal similar practices—of women who had two children, 16 percent of West German and 72 percent of East German women worked outside the home. For women with three children under the age of eighteen, the figures are 18 percent and 65 percent respectively.[30]

A daycare group in Vetschau, East Germany, plays outdoors with a massive power plant in the background in 1970. The East German government built day care centers in order to encourage mothers of young children to enter the paid workforce. Nearly a third of East German children between the ages of one and three were enrolled in such centers in 1970; nearly two-thirds of three- to six-year-olds were in kindergartens. bpk, Berlin / Photo: Max Ittenbach /Art Resource, NY

Work for women was increasingly viewed as a right, which became apparent when the East German regime was overturned with the reunification of East and West Germany after 1989. According to surveys, women in East Germany enjoyed being economically independent and defined themselves by the jobs they did, not as housewives and mothers. Interviews conducted in the mid-1990s confirmed women's appreciation of former East German policies regarding women's work. For example, a mother of two children who worked as a harbor traffic dispatcher in the port city of Rostock claimed:

> I liked working. I didn't study for nothing. It is a job that I enjoy. And during GDR times [that is, before unification] I could combine both children and career, that worked very well. And for that reason I don't want to stay home because I don't think I am the type, who can be at home all day. And then there is the financial factor too.[31]

Western claims to the contrary, women did not see state family policies in the East as coercive. In fact, women's choices in the realm of the family were broader than in West Germany. The state emphasized support and incentives rather than prohibitions. Contraception was widely available and women could choose to abort unwanted pregnancies up until the twelfth week of pregnancy. Although reported abortion rates were significantly higher than in the West, East German women still had more children than their Western counterparts in the last decades before reunification.[32]

China provides a different kind of example of a modern state that engaged in the surveillance, measurement, and management of human life. After the fall of the Qing dynasty in 1911, China was politically fragmented and in a more or less constant state of civil war. At the end of World War II, China was reunited under the leadership of the Communist Party. In the early days of the People's Republic, the state encouraged reproduction, on the theory that more citizens made for a stronger state. But it became increasingly apparent that the population was growing at a rate that would put a damper on economic growth. In 1979, the Chinese state decided to implement a policy that would limit most couples to having one child. This policy was very effective at reducing the birthrate, using a combination of coercion, persuasion, and rewards.

The details of the system varied with time and place, but in many places the intrusion of the state into women's bodies was extreme; in some areas, neighborhood cadres would compile information on what birth control methods married couples were using and when women had their menstrual periods, which made it easier to track early pregnancies. Second and subsequent children might be denied access to schooling, food rations, and the like, or they might be subject to substantial fines. With modern medical procedures such as ultrasound to inform prospective parents of the sex of their unborn child, sex-selective abortion and occasional abandonment of girl babies has resulted in skewed gender ratios. The Chinese patrilineal system assumes that sons will take care of their parents in their old age; in the absence of any systematic pension system, it is easy to see why many couples might prefer sons over daughters.

The one-child policy was never enforced as strongly in rural areas as it was in the cities. A resident of rural Guangdong, with three children and a fourth one on the way, told a *New York Times* reporter in 2000: "Oh yes, family planning is very strict here. . . . But fine me? There's no way. I'm a peasant and I don't really have any income. What can they

A 1980s poster advocates the Chinese one-child policy. The young mother with one child on her shoulder in front of a gleaming city makes clear the connection between family planning and state growth. International Institute of Social History, Chinese Posters, BG E13/415

do?"[33] Even in urban areas, governments relaxed policies a bit toward the end of the twentieth century; in most areas, if two people who were both the only children in their family married each other, they would be allowed to have a second child, in order to mitigate the problem of taking care of grandparents. But the gender imbalance has meant that a growing number of young men are unable to find wives. Some men who have not been able to find Chinese wives have married women from Southeast Asia, a ripple effect of the population policies of the Chinese state.

During the same time that Chinese government instituted its one-child policy, other countries instituted measures of population control as a way of increasing the living standard of their people. Sometimes coercive measures were used, as in India in the 1970s, when the government implemented policies of coerced sterilizations (and gave transistor radios as incentives to men who had vasectomies.)[34] In other parts of the world as well, population control was a key element in global power politics from the 1950s through the 1970s.

Family policies that had been promoted by colonial governments came under attack from anticolonial movements. For example, in Kenya, the practice of "female circumcision" (which its opponents more often call "female genital mutilation") came to be associated with nationalist movements that hoped to end colonial rule. Christian missionaries in the early part of the twentieth century had targeted this practice, part of girls' coming-of-age rituals in many regions of Kenya. The missionary campaign to eradicate it was thus linked to other aspects of colonial rule.

Given this history, then, it is not surprising that movements such as the Mau-Mau, who rose in rebellion against the British in Kenya in the 1950s, would insist that their adherents continue or reintroduce the practice and make sure to have their sons and daughter undergo these coming-of-age rituals. The continuing controversy over female circumcision is shown in the title of a 1999 article in *The Economist*—"Female Genital Mutilation: Is It Crime or Is It Culture?"[35]

Family ideals and metaphors also played into anticolonial nationalism in Vietnam. Prior to its colonization by the French in the late nineteenth century, Vietnam had been strongly influenced by Confucian ethics and family values. In the 1920s, French colonial administrators and educators, as well as Vietnamese intellectuals, began to discuss the question of the role of women in a changing society in ways that challenged Confucian family hierarchies. But the family remained and still remains central to Vietnamese conceptions of the nation.

French colonial authorities supported education for women, but they focused their efforts on education that would reinforce their family roles. One French colonial administrator wrote in a Vietnamese-language book in 1928 entitled *What Rural People Should Know* that a woman should be "nimble, clean, kitchen-wise, and proficient in sewing, and should even know how to read and write."[36] A Vietnamese-language textbook from the colonial era entitled *Female Citizen's Self-Instruction* promoted the idea that girls should be trained to be "mothers to the nation."[37] A textbook entitled *Reader for Female Students* asked "Unless you obey the words of your father and mother, how can you know how to obey the laws of the state?" suggesting a relationship between family and state that had its roots in both Confucian and more modern political rhetoric. In the early twentieth century, books on sexual hygiene introduced the modern vocabulary of eugenics and population improvement. For example, the connection between sexual hygiene and the development of the nation was made clear in a manual on pregnancy and infant diseases written by a Vietnamese physician in 1925; he wrote, "our race will day by day grow stronger when we finally pay attention to child care and the prevention of child-deforming illness."[38]

The French were able to fend off a growing nationalist movement through the first half of the twentieth century; they remained in power until the Japanese invasion in 1941. Nationalists, led by Ho Chi Minh and others, opposed both French and Japanese rule. After the Japanese were defeated in World War II, they left Vietnam, but the French did not. The French fought to retain control of the colony despite a declaration of independence by anticolonial rebels in 1945. The anticolonial leadership of Vietnam reasserted the values of filial piety, making it clear that what was at stake was not merely a reassertion of traditional Confucian ideas linking family and state loyalties but an imagination of a new future, with modern patriotic citizens. Ho Chi Minh wrote that "to defer to the claims of filial piety, to feel bound in duty and gratitude to virtuous exemplary forebears, [is] in keeping with the values of a modern patriot selflessly serving party, state and nation, exalting youth and progress, and looking fearlessly to the future."[39]

He continued the theme of looking to the future in an address to schoolchildren shortly after independence was declared in 1945:

> Previously, your fathers and older brothers, and last year still, you yourselves were forced to accept a slave's education, designed to train lackeys for the French imperialists. Today, you are luckier than your fathers and older brothers in being educated in an independent country. . . . Whether the Vietnamese nation can achieve glory, whether the Vietnamese people can become as glorious as the powerful countries of the five continents depends in large part on your efforts to educate yourselves.[40]

The theme of the future of the nation-state depending on its children is a recurrent one.

Vietnamese forces defeated the French, thus ending French colonial rule, in the First Indochina War in 1954. At the end of that war, Vietnam was divided into two states, North Vietnam and South Vietnam, with the dividing line at the seventeenth parallel. The north was ruled by a communist regime and the south by an anticommunist regime friendlier to the Western world. In the process of political division, some families were split, both geographically and ideologically. Like East and West Germany, divided Vietnam became a critical site in the Cold War. In the Second Indochina War, the American War in Vietnam, the United States intervened on the side of the south in its fight against the communist north. The war was long and bloody, and the United States ultimately was defeated in 1975. Vietnam was reunified under the communist north. Duong Van Mai Elliott underscores the connections between national and family reunification in her memoir. "Reunification made the population feel as one again. Families could be reunited, and ties that had been severed were re-established."[41] An iconic emblem of political reunification, a photo of a mother embracing her son, distributed as a poster and widely published in newspapers, suggests ways in which the pain of the division of Vietnam into north and south was seen as a family tragedy and the reunification was seen as a family reunion.[42]

In the post-reunification years, Vietnam's economy prospered, leading to its designation as one of the "Little Asian Tiger" economies. In 1986, the government instituted a series of reforms designed to institute a socialist-driven market economy. Under conditions of peace and growing prosperity, the population has continued to grow, and the Vietnamese government, like those elsewhere, has involved itself more directly in family matters. In 1988, the government instituted a plan to limit births to two children per woman. As in China, the pressure has resulted in gender imbalances, with families preferring boys to girls. By 2009, there were 115 male births for every 100 female births.[43] This preference suggests that, as in China, older family ideals have persisted despite government efforts to modernize the family.

Further evidence of this persistence comes from folk songs like one still sung in rural areas in the 1990s: "Your daughter is a child of the other /Only a daughter-in-law is your daughter since you have paid for her." The song refers both to patrilineal marriage customs (girls become members of the families of their husbands) and the custom of the family of the bride paying a bride price.[44]

Not only have population policies aimed to restrict the number of births, they have also sought to increase the "quality" of babies born. In 2009, the head of the Vietnamese General Office for Population and Family Planning, Dr. Duong Quoc Trong, "stressed that the most important duty of the authorities in future is to enhance the population quality by reducing the number of children with congenital malformations to below 1.5 percent." Trong does not actually say what the authorities are supposed to do to accomplish this end, but there is a strong suggestion that both better prenatal care and coerced abortions could be considered. He also points to more forceful government intervention in response to the sex ratio problem, indicating that "it is very difficult for Vietnam to prevent the imbalance in the sex ratio if the country just depends on education and propaganda. The government should have stricter sanctions on those not complying with the law."[45]

The impulses and consequences of state policies affecting families have varied tremendously from one regime to another, sometimes serving democratization and sometimes serving authoritarian and even genocidal goals. In Nazi Germany, state policy aimed to increase the number of "pure" German families. In modernizing China, the one-child rule was fundamental in restricting rapid population growth. In East and West Germany, varying state policies regarding female participation in the paid labor force had clear consequences for family life. In Vietnam, different family policies marked the transition from colonial to postcolonial regimes. By the end of the twentieth century, the family had become politicized in virtually every region and state of the world.

Epilogue:
The Future of the Family

The evolution of family life continues to shape, and be shaped by, historical forces. Now more than ever, these changes take place in a global framework. The deep history of the family—reaching back to the earliest emergence of the human species—has left its imprint on global historical processes. Humans everywhere descend from common ancestors who evolved in the social context of domestic relationships. However, for many thousands of years, family histories have diverged as diasporas and reencounters across cultures have created distinctive ways of living in families.

In our contemporary world of dense global communications, migration has a somewhat different impact on family life than it did in the past, but it is an incontrovertible influence on many families. Migration shapes societies on both sides of migrant streams. In the past, the long treks or ocean voyages that migration often entailed meant that a departure might be forever. Family mementos or letters carried or sent by migrants are poignant reminders of some migrants' efforts to maintain the bonds of family over long distances. Just to offer one example, in 1956 Anna Paikens wrote from her home in Latvia to her son Edward, who had settled in Minnesota after World War II as a displaced person:

> Little Maija studies Russian and German at school . . . She has tried to find on the map the city that you live in and she says that it is very far. She showed me on the map that one centimeter is 1000 kilometers. It appears more than 20,000 kilometers away. Son if you will send me something, send me some big and medium size and also some small needles for my Singer sewing machine. The other day I forgot to ask you. My most endearing greetings you. The same to Helena.
>   All the best,
>   Mother
>   P.S.—Greetings also from Maija. She can't wait to receive a letter from you.[1]

Paikens' letter evokes the enormous distance that separated her from her son but also their efforts to connect over everyday activities like sewing and schoolwork. Now, communication technology—air travel, cheap phone calls, social media, webcams—means that connections among members of globally migrant families can involve a "daily life" flavor that was much more difficult when letters took a long time and phone calls were not yet possible or were very expensive—or, in even earlier eras, when an overseas departure meant the end of all communications. Now family ties can persist across space to an unprecedented extent. But it's important to keep in mind the vulnerability of those ties in a world still ruled by nation-states with their enormous capacity to shape the conditions of family life, including how people move within and across borders. Our contemporary globalized world is also a world where families are often threatened by a widespread suspicion of immigrants or broken apart by deportation.

In many realms of contemporary "family history in the making," there are simultaneously local or national as well as transnational or global forces at play. Sexual orientation is one important new frontier in terms of the future of family. Although monogamous heterosexual unions are seen as the norm throughout much of the modern world, a variety of modes of family formation and alternative sexualities have been recognized in many cultures. Levels of prevalence or tolerance of such alternatives have depended on dramatically varying cultural interpretations of what constitutes a proper family life and degrees of political support or repression of forms of family outside the norms.

The most visible form of challenge to prevailing family relations in many regions of the world today is the gay rights movement and the related call by some gay rights activists for the recognition of same-sex marriages and adoption rights for gay couples. Increasingly, political movements such as gay rights operate in a realm that is global rather than restricted to one locality. In 2006, South Africa became the first country in Africa to recognize gay marriage and the fifth country in the world to do so. It is now illegal in South Africa for any organization to discriminate against any of the newly recognized forms of marriage or partnership. The South African model has been important for gay rights advocates elsewhere in the world. For example, the Los Angeles–based columnist and gay rights activist Carl Matthes wrote in 2010 that despite its ongoing problems, South Africa offers "a model for the future."[2]

But gay marriage politics depend on local politics too. In the United States, there have been debates over gay marriage and legal challenges in individual states for decades. Legal battles over gay marriage have brought historians of the family directly into the courtroom; historical evidence in these cases has become legal evidence. For example, in 2003,

Massachusetts Supreme Court Justice Margaret Marshall's ruling in the case of *Goodridge v. Department of Public Health* (which overturned the state's ban on same-sex marriage) drew on an amicus brief signed by dozens of historians. The brief argued explicitly that the meaning of marriage and legal relationships constituted by it have changed over time. Legal relations between husbands and wives within marriage have changed dramatically, as women are no longer considered legal minors, for one thing; another example the brief offered was that interracial marriage is no longer prohibited and punished as it formerly was throughout much of the United States.[3] Cases like this one have made explicit both the political and historical nature of marriage and the highly contentious nature of the issues raised by its reform.

Demands for gay marriage involve religious dimensions as well. While many of the opponents of gay marriage in the United States and elsewhere base their opposition on religious prescriptions and scriptural injunctions that have long figured heavily in shaping family values, not all organized religions take a stand against gay marriage. For example, by a recent decision, a Minneapolis Friends (Quaker) meeting decided not to marry anyone until they could marry everyone—they will continue to have commitment ceremonies for same-sex and heterosexual couples, but they will not sign the official marriage certificates that are as of now according to Minnesota law only available to heterosexual couples. "We're simply trying to be consistent with the will of God as we perceive it," said Paul Landskroener, clerk of the Twin Cities Friends Meeting, in a December 2009 interview.[4] These debates over gay marriage, and underlying anxieties about the nature of marriage as a social institution more generally, are one important indication of the ongoing nature of family history.

Another important innovation in family life that holds implications for the future of the family is reproductive technology, especially the combination of genetic engineering and surrogacy contracts. In the past, couples (or, more rarely, individuals) who wished for children but were not able themselves to have children biologically could adopt. Now, beyond adoption, childless people can also choose to hire a woman— called a surrogate—to bear a child for them. Sometimes the egg and sperm are donated by the couple; increasingly, however, the egg and sperm are handpicked from "products" made available by commercial firms that promise offspring with desired genetic traits. Strictly speaking, traffic in human beings has long been outlawed in national and international law, but some forms of implementation of these new technologies of reproduction come uncomfortably close to recreating it in a new form.

In a 2009 interview with a reporter for the *New York Times*, parents involved in a dispute over twin babies born though a surrogacy contract claimed their parental rights in market terms: "We paid for the egg, the sperm, the in vitro fertilization . . . They wouldn't be here if it weren't for us."[5] In the United States, there are as yet relatively few states that regulate surrogacy, whether commercial or not. Most European countries and several other countries either regulate surrogacy or outlaw it completely. While there is of course no claim that reproduction through surrogacy is innately flawed or will result in dramatically different family dynamics, the commercial character of much surrogacy raises moral, ethical, and legal issues.

In the absence of state regulation, the fertility clinics, genetic laboratories, and surrogate mothers who stand to profit from the business are left to control conditions of their own operation without any regulation. The possibility of contracting with someone else to produce a child with commercially supplied genetic materials, according to bioethicist George J. Annas, runs the risk of "seeing children as a consumer product . . . It really does treat children like commodities. Like pets."[6]

Not that adoption is unproblematic either, since family values and the politics of the family always intervene in determining which children are available for adoption and which potential parents are deemed suitable. Adoption agencies have long wielded considerable control over who could and could not adopt; many of the people who have children through surrogates would have had difficulty adopting because of their age, health, marital status, or sexual orientation. In a globalized world of adoption, things are even more complicated. The politics of adoption are transnational, and adoption now often entails negotiating international laws and agencies as well as the ethics of transferring children from poorer to richer world regions and dramatic cross-cultural differences between birth and adoptive families.

"Star" adoptions and transnational charities have brought the ethics of transnational policy regarding orphans into the limelight and called attention to various approaches to caring for large numbers of orphans, an increasing number of whose parents have died as a result of warfare or AIDS epidemics. Attempts to support children locally are sometimes at odds with the demands of the international "adoption market." Forms of international aid hold implications for how orphaned children are treated. While some administrators favor well-endowed orphanages such as the Home of Hope in Malawi, which is supported by the singer Madonna, others are more skeptical that isolated acts by celebrities can solve widespread problems. Throughout African regions affected by

AIDS, most orphans are in fact taken in by extended family members; this may be better for them in the long run, but there is relatively little state support or international charity to come to their aid. As in so many other realms of the family of the future, the interplay of the local and the global are visible.

When we look at relationships between the family and the state, especially family welfare policies, we can see dramatic differences, which again highlight the historical processes of family history in the making. One striking example is in the realm of reproductive health care. Though both the United States and France are wealthy countries, the resources available to women are strikingly different. In the United States, provisions will change as the implications of the new health care system are worked out. But as of 2010, reproductive health coverage was very uneven; nearly half of the states did not require health plans to include coverage for contraceptives. In a state like Colorado, for example, women have had to pay out of pocket for contraception, and often for maternity care as well. The provisions regarding reproductive health were among the most controversial in the 2009–10 debates over health care reform.

France presents an interesting contrast, and most European countries are more like France than the United States. France is deemed by many experts to offer the best public support for reproductive health. Not only are all costs associated with contraception and abortion routinely covered by the state's generous health care plan, so too is maternity and postnatal care. New mothers get several months of paid leave as well as child allowances and access to free neighborhood clinics and home nurse programs, as well as subsidized day care.

At the other end of the life course, the situation of older people and state provision for elder care are also a new frontier of family life. As life expectancies rise throughout much of the world, families face new constellations of cross-generational relationships. In a recent article in a British newspaper, one woman remarked, "It's wise to have children while your mother's still young enough to look after them."[7] Her comment reflected her position—similar to that of many middle-aged women in Britain and throughout Europe and beyond—who find themselves caught between the need to care for their parents on one hand and their children on the other.

This "sandwich generation" phenomenon has become increasingly common in those societies where women are active in the labor force and delay childbearing into their thirties or even forties. With life expectancy rising at the same time, they are often caring for young children and aging parents at the same time. In Great Britain, for example, about 10 percent of the population has significant responsibility for an elderly parent; a million Britons are simultaneously caring for both children and elderly family members. Most of these caretakers are also in the paid workforce. This situation is on the radar screen of policymakers in many countries with similar demographic profiles. There is increasing interest in policies that will provide options to support family and community caregivers, and thus to present alternatives to institutionalization for the growing number of older people. The options that will attract increasing attention will no doubt include forms of support that will allow grown children to combine caring for elders with the other demands of family and workplace.

Elder care presents a special challenge in contemporary society because of earlier population control policies. As a result of the Chinese single-child policy enforced in the 1980s and 1990s as a means of encouraging faster economic development through restricting population growth, a new dilemma presented itself by the beginning of the twenty-first century: there are relatively few young people to care for the large number of elders. This is known in China as the "4-2-1 problem"—four grandparents (two married couples) together produced only two children, who in turn produced only one grandchild. How can one third-generation child take care of four grandparents? How does a married couple take care of eight grandparents for whom they are the sole descendants, and also work and raise their own child? As a result of the 4-2-1 problem, the Chinese government has been forced to rethink and revise the one-child policy. The precise rules vary at the provincial level; recently, for example, it has been considered permissible for people who are themselves single children who marry single children to have more than one child, so that the one child won't then have to take care of eight great-grandparents, should they live so long. This is a special form of the problem of rethinking elder care that families face all over the world as a result of rising life expectancies and changing forms of family life.

The construction of "global families" through migration and adoption, political challenges that seek to redefine what a family is and how a family is formed, new technologies that are dramatically altering reproduction, demographic patterns that are shifting generational power relations—these are just a few examples of contemporary dynamics that illustrate how family life and ideas about the family will shape the future even as they have shaped the past.

Chronology

100,000 BCE–70,000 BCE
Earliest evidence of *Homo sapiens* cognitive abilities such as the use of language and the construction of symbolic objects, allowing the transmission of knowledge and memory from generation to generation

10,000 BCE–7000 BCE
Earliest evidence of permanent human settlements and the domestication of plants and animals in Eurasia and the Americas

3000 BCE
Clear evidence of Mesopotamian urban centers and first historically recorded state systems

3000 BCE
Earliest Egyptian dynastic state; evidence of Egyptian deities and relations between deities and pharaohs

1750 BCE
Creation of the Code of Hammurabi, the earliest known complete law code

First millennium BCE
Writing of *The Laws of Manu,* which codifies beliefs dating back to the second millennium

800–500 BCE
Writing of the earliest books of the Old Testament, the scriptural basis for ancient Judaism and, later, Christianity

551 BCE
Birth of Confucius, according to most sources; foundation of the formalization of Chinese ethical and spiritual thought into the system later named Confucianism

Fifth century BCE
First texts on the life of the Buddha begin to circulate, though they are not recorded until the first century BCE

221–207 BCE
Unification of China under the Qin Dynasty, the first imperial dynasty

Sixth through fifth centuries BCE
Flourishing of the city-state of Athens; experimentation with democratic rather than dynastic rule

33 CE
Death of Jesus Christ, followed by circulation of his teachings by disciples and the foundation of the Christian religion

First through tenth centuries CE
Classic period of the Maya, emergence of state system in Central America

632 CE
Death of the prophet Muhammad, followed by the spread of his teachings

800 CE
Foundation by Charlemagne of the Holy Roman Empire in Western and Central Europe, associated with the Christianization of Europe and the emergence of distinct ecclesiastical and secular systems of family and other types of law

1000 CE
Civil service examination system instituted in China; mastering Confucian classics established as a meritocratic route to state office

1100 CE
City of Timbuktu emerges

Late 13th to early 19th centuries
Use of the janissary system in the Ottoman Empire

1415–1605
First wave of European colonial adventures in Africa, Asia, and the New World

1492
King Ferdinand and Queen Isabella unite Spain under a single monarchy; first of a series of edicts eventually leading to the forced conversion or expulsion of Jews and Muslims from Spain; first voyage of Columbus

1494

Start of European missionary activities in New World, launch of new wave of missions around the world

1517

Luther launches a critique of Catholic views of salvation that leads to the beginning of the Protestant Reformation

1526–1860

Atlantic slave trade took millions of captured and enslaved Africans to the New World

1545–1563

Meeting of the Council of Trent, as part of the Catholic response to the Reformation

1582

First Jesuit missions in China

1690–1800

Publication of major Enlightenment-era treatises on family, education, and socialization, as well as critiques of dynastic rule, including the Baron Montesquieu's *Persian Letters* and *The Spirit of the Laws,* Jean-Jacques Rousseau's *Emile,* and Mary Wollstonecraft's *Vindication of the Rights of Woman*

1733

Invention of the flying shuttle in England by John Kay, first of a series of inventions, including the spinning jenny (1770) and the steam engine (1775), designed to improve productivity and profitability in cotton manufacture; these inventions led to the Industrial Revolution

1789–1815

French Revolution and Napoleonic era; establishment in and beyond Europe of new relationships between state and citizenry and new family law codes

1800–1830

Beginning of massive migrations across Atlantic and Pacific Oceans that bring people from Europe and Asia to the Americas, ushering in a new era of transnational family life

1870

Beginning of second wave of European colonization of Africa and Asia

1911–1919

Overthrow of Qing dynasty and May Fourth Movement in China, which made idea of family reform central to political progress

1922–1945

Domination of fascism, Nazism, and related regimes in Europe; implementation of racialist policies such as marriage limitations, sterilization, and annihilation of people deemed racially inferior

1945–1989

Family forms implicated in competition between Western bloc and Soviet bloc

1946–1964

Postwar baby boom in the United States

1948–1997

Period of decolonization; independence of former European colonies in Africa and Asia

1960

Birth control pill becomes available in the United States

1969

Publication of article on "test tube babies" and beginnings of human artificial insemination as standard medical practice in many Western countries

1979

Introduction of the "one-child policy" in the People's Republic of China

2001

The Netherlands becomes the first state to allow gay marriage, followed by others; ongoing debates over gay marriage between state and church

Notes

PREFACE

1. Daniel Smail, *On Deep History and the Brain* (Berkeley: University of California Press, 2008); *David Christian, Maps of Time: An Introduction to Big History* (Berkeley: University of California Press, 2004); Mary Jo Maynes and Ann Waltner, "Temporalities and Periodization in Deep History: Technology, Gender, and Benchmarks of 'Human Development,'" *Social Science History* 36:1 (2012): 59–83.

CHAPTER 1

1. Ian Hodder, "This Old House," *Natural History* 115 (2006): 42–47.
2. Johann Bachofen, *Mutterrecht*, originally published in1861. For a full discussion of this history, see Ann Taylor Allen, "Feminism, Social Science and the Meanings of Modernity: The Debate on the Origin of the Family in Europe and the United States," *American Historical Review* 104 (1999): 1085–113.
3. The evidence continues to be debated. For an analysis of these questions, see Diane Bolger, "Gender and Human Evolution" and "A Critical Appraisal of Gender Research in African Archaeology," in *Handbook of Gender in Archaeology,* edited by Sarah Milledge Nelson (Lanham, MD: Altamira Press, 2006), 453–501 and 595–631.
4. See discussion in Michael Cook, *A Brief History of the Human Race* (New York: W.W. Norton, 2005), pp. 21–25.
5. Michael Balter, "Plant Science: Seeking Agriculture's Ancient Roots," *Science* 319 (2007): 1830–35.
6. Heather Pringle, "Neolithic Agriculture: The Slow Birth of Agriculture," *Science* 282 (1998): 1446.
7. David Christian, *Maps of Time: An Introduction to Big History* (Berkeley: University of California Press, 2004), 223–24.
8. See the discussion in Jared Diamond, *Guns, Germs and Steel* (New York: W.W. Norton, 1997), especially chapters 6 and 11.
9. Diane Lyons, "A Critical Appraisal of Gender Research in African Archaeology," in *Worlds of Gender: The Archaeology of Women's Lives around the Globe,* edited by Sarah Milledge Nelson (Lanham, MD: Altamira Press, 2007), 12–13.
10. Hetty Jo Brumbach and Robert Jarvenpa, "Gender Dynamics in Hunter-Gatherer Societies: Archeological Methods and Perspectives," in *Handbook of Gender in Archaeology,* edited by Nelson, 520–22.
11. Lyons, 13.
12. Ruth Whitehouse, "Gender Archaeology in Europe," in *Handbook of Gender in Archaeology,* edited by Nelson, 744.
13. This and all subsequent descriptions of Çatalhöyük are from Hodder, "This Old House."
14. Qiang Gao and Yun Kuen Lee, "A Biological Perspective on Yangshao Kinship," *Journal of Anthropological Archaeology* 12 (1993): 266–98.
15. Gideon Shelach, "Marxist and Post-Marxist Paradigms for the Neolithic," in *Gender and Chinese Archaeology,* edited by Kathryn Linduff (Lanham, MD: Altamira Press, 2004), 21.
16. Gao and Lee, 273.

17. Virginia Ebert and Thomas C. Patterson, "Gender in South American Archaeology," in *Handbook of Gender in Archaeology,* edited by Nelson, 860–61.

18. Ruth Shady Solis, Jonathan Haas, and Winifred Creamer, "Dating Caral, a Preceramic Site in the Supe Valley," *Science,* 292 (2001): 723–26.

CHAPTER 2

1. See Ian Tattersall, *The World from Beginnings to 4000 BCE* (New York: Oxford University Press, 2008), 89–108.

2. Alister Doyle, "Botswana 'Snake Rock' May Show Stone Age Religion," *The Namibian,* December 4, 2006, accessed February 11, 2011, http://www.namibian.com.na/index. php?id=28&tx_ttnews[tt_news]=22763&;no_cache=1.

3. Bettina Arnold, "Gender and Archaeological Mortuary Analysis," in *Handbook of Gender in Archaeology,* edited by Nelson, 137–70.

4. Cook, *A Brief History of the Human Race,* 51–52, 110.

5. Bettina Arnold, "Gender, Temporalities and Periodization in Iron Age West-Central Europe," *Social Science History* 36:1 (forthcoming, spring 2012)

6. "The Story of Isis and Osiris," Ancient Egypt: The Mythology, last modified April 21, 2001, accessed September 27, 2011, http://www.egyptianmyths.net/mythisis.htm.

7. Barbara Watterson, *Women in Ancient Egypt* (New York: St. Martin's Press, 1991), 21.

8. Karl Taube, *Aztec and Maya Myths* (London: British Museum Press, 1993), 57–58.

9. Genesis (King James Version), accessed September 27, 2011 http://quod.lib.umich.edu/ cgi/k/kjv/kjv-idx?type=DIV1&;byte=1477.

10. Gerda Lerner, *The Creation of Patriarchy* (New York: Oxford University Press, 1987), 168–80.

11. Lerner, 170.

12. Cook, *A Brief History of the Human Race,* 65–69.

13. Brian Peter Harvey, *An Introduction to Buddhism* (Cambridge University Press, 1990), 140.

14. Wendy Doniger with Brian Smith, *The Laws of Manu* (New York: Penguin, 1991), 3.

15. Doniger, 115–16.

16. See Leila Ahmed, *Women and Gender in Islam: Historical Roots of a Modern Debate* (New Haven: Yale University Press, 1992).

17. Quoted in Ahmed, 65.

18. Ahmed, 49–52.

19. Ahmed, 76.

20. Ahmed, 84.

21. Ahmed, 87.

22. *Life of the Buddha by Aśvaghoṣa* translated by Patrick Olivelle (New York: New York University Press, 2008), 5.

23. *Life of the Buddha,* 233.

24. *Life of the Buddha,* 249.

25. *Life of the Buddha,* 255.

26. A good introduction to this story is Stephen Teiser, *The Ghost Festival in Medieval China* (Princeton: Princeton University Press, 1988).

27. Galatians 3:28, accessed September 27, 2011 AppData/Local/Temp/%3Ca href=http:// quod.lib.umich.edu/cgi/k/kjv/kjv-idx?type=DIV1&;byte=1477.

28. Luke 14:25–35 and 18:28–30, accessed September 27, 2011 AppData/Local/Temp/%3Ca href=http://quod.lib.umich.edu/cgi/k/kjv/kjv-idx?type=DIV1&;byte=1477.

29. Ahmed, 36.

30. Augustine, "On Marriage," §6, Women can be Priests, accessed September 27, 2011, http://www.womenpriests.org/traditio/august.asp#venial.

31. Tertullian, *De Cultu Feminarum*, Book 1, Chapter 1, and "An Exhortation to Chastity," Chapter 9, Women can be Priests, accessed September 27, 2011, http://www.womenpriests.org/traditio/tertul.asp.

32. For a collection of these sources, see Sebastien Brock and Susan Harvey, editors, *Holy Women of the Syrian Orient* (Berkeley: University of California Press, 1987).

33. Quoted in Ahmed, 23.

CHAPTER 3

1. Lerner, *The Creation of Patriarchy*, 66–67.

2. Lerner, 56–57.

3. Lerner, 108.

4. Herodotus, *The Histories. Second Book: An Account of Egypt*, translated by G. C. Macaulay, accessed September 27, 2011, http://www.gutenberg.org/files/2131/2131-h/2131-h.htm.

5. Watterson, *Women in Ancient Egypt*, 24–25.

6. Watterson, 31.

7. Watterson, 30–31.

8. Lana Troy, "She for Whom All is Said and Done: The Ancient Egyptian Queen," in *Ancient Queens: Archaeological Explorations,* edited by Sarah Milledge Nelson (Lanham, MD: Altamira Press, 2003), 93–116.

9. J. Katherine Josserand, "Women in Classic Maya Hieroglyphic Texts," in *Ancient Maya Women,* edited by Traci Ardren (Walnut Creek, CA: Altamira Press, 2002), 121–22.

10. Karen Olsen Bruhns, "Yesterday the Queen Wore . . . An Analysis of Women and Costume in the Public Art of the Late Classic Maya," in *The Role of Gender in Precolumbian Art and Architecture*, edited by Virginia E. Miller (Lanham, MD: University Press of America, 1988), 111, 134.

11. Sarah B. Pomeroy, *Goddesses, Whores, Wives, and Slaves* (New York: Schocken Books, 1995), 57.

12. Pomeroy, 65.

13. Gerald R. Hawting, *The First Dynasty of Islam: The Umayyad Caliphate AD 661–750* (London: Psychology Press, 2000), 13.

14. Elias N. Saad, *Social History of Timbuktu: The Role of Muslim Scholars and Notables, 1400–1900* (Cambridge: Cambridge University Press, 1983), 27.

15. Leo Africanus, "The Description of Africa," African-American Heritage and Ethnography, accessed October 4, 2011, http://www.nps.gov/history/ethnography/aah/aaheritage/histContexts_pop1.htm.

16. Saad, 89.

17. Saad, 69–70.

18. Saad, 79.

19. Saad, 236.

20. Joan Baxter, "The Treasures of Timbuktu," *The Star* (Timbuktu, Mali), December 18, 2005.

21. Lydia Polgreen, "Timbuktu Hopes Ancient Texts Spark a Revival," *New York Times,* August 7, 2007.

CHAPTER 4

1. Susan Kellogg, *Law and Transformation of the Aztec Culture* (University of Oklahoma Press, 2005), 202.

2. Kellogg, 203.

3. Ibn Battuta, *Travels in Asia and Africa 1325–1354*, translated and edited by H. A. R. Gibb (London: Broadway House, 1929), Internet Medieval Sourcebook, accessed September 27, 2011, http://www.fordham.edu/halsall/source/1354-ibnbattuta.html.

4. Ibid.

5. *The First Letter of Christopher Columbus to the Noble Lord Raphael Sanchez Announcing the Discovery of America* (Boston: Published by the Trustees, 1891), p. 13, Open Library, accessed September 27, 2011, http://www.archive.org/stream/firstletterofchr00colu#page/n7/mode/2up.

6. *The Ain I Akbari by Abul Fazl `Allami,* translated by H. Blochmann (Asiatic Society of Bengal, Calcutta: Printed by G.H. Rouse at the Baptist Mission Press, 1873), Vol. I, p.44, accessed February 12, 2011, http://persian.packhum.org/persian/main?url=pf%3Ffile%3D00702050%26ct%3D0.

7. Ruby Lal, *Domesticity and Power in the Early Mughal World* (Cambridge and New York: Cambridge University Press, 2005), 173; Rosalind O'Hanlon, "Kingdom, Household and Body History, Gender and Imperial Service under Akbar," *Modern Asian Studies* 41:5 (2007): 889–923.

8. "Christopher Columbus: Extracts from Journal," edited by Robert Guisepi, 2002, originally published in John Fiske, *Discovery of America,* Appendix C (Boston and New York: Houghton Mifflin, 1892), accessed September 27, 2011, http://history-world.org/christopherdocs.htm.

9. Quoted in Lyndal Roper, "Luther: Sex, Marriage, and Motherhood," *History Today* 33 (1983): 12, 33.

10. Martin Luther, "The Estate of Marriage (1522)," translated by Walther I. Brandt, in *Luther's Works,* edited by Helmut T. Lehmann, vol. 45, *The Christian in Society* (Philadelphia: Fortress Press, 1962), 38–46.

11. Lucia Ferrante, "Marriage and Women's Subjectivity in a Patrilineal System: The Case of Early Modern Bologna," in *Gender, Kinship, Power: A Comparative and Interdisciplinary History*, ed. Mary Jo Maynes et al. (New Brunswick: Routledge Press, 1996), 115–29.

12. Mark A. Burkholder with Suzanne Hiles, "An Empire beyond Compare," in *The Oxford History of Mexico*, edited by Michael C. Meyerand and William H. Beezley (Oxford: Oxford University Press, 2000), 127.

13. Robert S. Haskett, "Living in Two Worlds: Cultural Continuity and Change among Curenavaca's Indigenous Elite," *Ethnohistory* 35 (1988): 34–59; Patricia Seed, *To Love, Honor and Obey in Colonial Mexico: Conflicts over Marriage Choice, 1574–1821* (Stanford, CA: Stanford University Press, 1992).

14. Haskett, 39–40.

15. Merry Wiesner et al., *Discovering the Global Past: A Look at the Evidence*, 2nd ed. (Boston: Wadsworth, 2001), 430.

CHAPTER 5

1. Kaori O'Connor, "The King's Christmas Pudding: Globalization, Recipes, and the Commodities of Empire," *Journal of Global History* (2009) 4: 127–55.

2. Quoted in Daviken Studnicki-Gizbert, *A Nation upon the Ocean Sea: Portugal's Atlantic Diaspora and the Crisis of the Spanish Empire, 1492–1640* (New York: Oxford University Press, 2007), 85.

3. Susil Chaudhury, "Trading Networks in a Traditional Diaspora: Armenians in India, c. 1600–1800," in *Diaspora Entrepreneurial Networks,* 67. Diaspora Entrepreneurial Networks Four Centuries of History (2005) Publisher: Oxford, Berg, 2005, Pages: 51–72.

4. Jewish Women's Archive, Mariam Bodian, "Doña Gracia Nasi," accessed September 27, 2011, http://jwa.org/encyclopedia/article/nasi-dona-gracia.

5. Cecil Roth, *The House of Nasi: Doña Gracia* (Philadelphia: The Jewish Publication Society of America, 1948), 58.

6. Samuel Kurinsky, "The da Costas; a Remarkable Sephardic Family," Hebrew History Federation, accessed September 27, 2011, http://www.hebrewhistory.org/factpapers/40dacostas.html.

7. All examples of Portuguese Sephardic households from Daviken Studnicki-Gizbert, "*La Nación* among the Nations," in Richard L. Kagan and Philip D. Morgan, eds., *Atlantic Diasporas: Jews, Conversos, and Crypto-Jews in the Age of Mercantilism, 1500–1800* (Baltimore: JHU Press, 2009), 75–98.

8. Derek Nurse and Thomas Spear, *The Swahili: Reconstructing the History and Language of an African Society, 800–1500* (Philadelphia: University of Pennsylvania Press, 1985), 70–71.

9. Anthony Reid, "Diaspora Networks in the Asian Maritime Context," in *Diaspora Entrepreneurial Networks: Four Centuries of History,* edited by Ina Baghdiantz McCabe, Gelina Harlaftis, and Ioanna Pepelasis Minoglou (New York: Berg, 2005), 356.

10. Barbara Watson Andaya. "From Temporary Wife to Prostitute: Sexuality and Economic Change in Early Modern Southeast Asia." *Journal of Women's History* 9, no. 4 (1998): 11–34.

11. William D. Wray, "The Seventeenth-Century Japanese Diaspora: Questions of Boundary and Policy," in *Diaspora Entrepreneurial Networks,* edited by McCabe, Harlaftis, and Minoglou, 87–88.

12. Cemal Kafadar, "A History of Coffee," paper presented at Economic History Congress XIII, Buenos Aires, 2002.

13. See the data assembled in http://www.slavevoyages.org/tast/assessment/estimates.faces, accessed September 19, 2011. The co-Principal Investigatorss on the database project are David Eltis and Martin Halbert, both of Emory University.

14. From Basil Davidson, *The African Past* (London: Curtis Brown, 1964), 191–94. Cited in Wiesner et al., *Discovering the Global Past*, vol. 2, 42–43.

15. Harriet Jacobs, *Incidents in the Life of a Slave Girl Written by Herself,* edited by Lydia Maria Francis Child, 28, http://docsouth.unc.edu/fpn/jacobs/menu.html.

16. Jacobs, 47–48.

17. Ingeborg Weber-Kellermann, *Die Familie: Geschichte, Geschichten und Bilder* (Frankfurt am Main: Insel Verlag, 1976), 238.

18. Hans Medick, *Weben und Überleben in Laichingen 1650–1900: Lokalgeschichte als allgemeine Geschichte* (Göttingen: Max-Planck-Institut für Geschichte, 1996), 441–43.

19. Cited in Lutz Berkner, "The Stem Family and the Developmental Cycle of the Peasant Household: An Eighteenth-Century Austrian Example," *The American Historical Review* 77 (1972): 398–418.

CHAPTER 6

1. Anna Altmann, "Blätter und Blüten" [Leaves and Blossoms], in *Gedenkbuch: 20 Jahre österreichische Arbeiterinnenbewegung,* edited by Adelheid Popp (Vienna, 1912), 23–35. Translated by Mary Jo Maynes.

2. Maxine Berg, "What Difference did Women's Work Make to the Industrial Revolution?" in *Women's Work: The English Experience, 1650–1914,* edited by Pamela Sharpe (London: Arnold, 1998), 161.

3. Tom Hunt, *Portrait of an Industrial Village and Its Cotton Industry* (Dublin and Portland, OR: Irish Academic Press, 2000), 59–61.

4. Edward J. Watherston, "French Silk Manufactures, and the Industrial Employment of Women," *Good Words* 20 (1879): 110.

5. Friedrich Engels, *The Condition of the Working-Class in England in 1844* (London: Swan Sonnenschein & Co., 1892), 108; Project Gutenberg, accessed October 1, 2011, http://www.gutenberg.org/files/17306/17306-h/17306-h.htm.

6. Ibid.

7. These records are discussed in Bonnie Smith, *Ladies of the Leisure Class: The Bourgeoises of Northern France in the Nineteenth Century* (Princeton: Princeton University Press, 1981), 64.

8. Cited in Mary Jo Maynes, *Taking the Hard Road: Life Course in French and German Workers' Autobiographies in the Era of Industrialization* (Chapel Hill: The University of North Carolina Press, 1995), 74–75.

9. Charles de Secondat, Baron de Montesquieu, *The Spirit of Laws*, translated by Thomas Nugent, revised by J. V. Prichard (London: G. Bell & Sons, 1914), Vol. I, 6.

10. Excerpt from Jean-Jacques Rousseau, *Emile,* Women in World History Curriculum, accessed October 1, 2011, http://www.womeninworldhistory.com/lesson16.html.

11. See Lynn Hunt, *The Family Romance of the French Revolution* (Berkeley, CA: University of California Press, 1993).

12. Olympe de Gouges, "Declaration of the Rights of Woman," in *The French Revolution and Human Rights: A Brief Documentary History,* translated, edited, and with an introduction by Lynn Hunt (Boston/New York: Bedford/St. Martin's, 1996), 124–29. Downloaded at: http://chnm.gmu.edu/revolution/d/293/.

13. Wollstonecraft, *Vindication.*

14. See Suzanne Desan, *The Family on Trial in Revolutionary France* (Berkeley and Los Angeles: University of California Press, 2004).

15. Cited and translated in Jonathan Spence, *The Search for Modern China* (New York: Norton, 1990), 236.

16. Emily Honig, *Sisters and Strangers: Women in the Shanghai Cotton Mills* (Stanford: Stanford University Press, 1992).

17. Honig, 185.

18. Wiesner, *Discovering the Global Past,* vol. II, 86.

19. Susan Glosser, *Chinese Visions of Family and State, 1915–1953* (Berkeley: University of California Press 2003), 149.

20. Susan Fernsebner, "A People's Playthings: Toys, Childhood and Chinese Identity, 1909–33," *Postcolonial Studies* 6 (2003): 269–70.

CHAPTER 7

1. Michelle Mouton, *From Nurturing the Nation to Purifying the Volk: Weimar and Nazi Family Policy, 1918–1945* (Cambridge: Cambridge University Press, 2007), 144–45.

2. Mouton, 144.

3. Mouton, 139–40.

4. Margaret Llewelyn Davies, ed. *Maternity: Letters from Working Women,* reprint, with a new introduction, of the 1915 edition (New York: Norton, 1978), 53–54.

5. Quoted in Patrick Brantlinger, *Rule of Darkness: British Literature and Imperialism, 1830–1914* (Ithaca: Cornell University Press, 1990), 34.

6. Patricia M. E. Lorcin, *Historicizing Colonial Nostalgia: European Women's Narratives of Algeria and Kenya 1900-Present,* (New York: Palgrave Macmillan, 2012), 74.

7. Conklin, 79.

8. Eric Weitz, "Before the Holocaust: Germany and Genocide in Africa and Anatolia," unpublished MS, p. 13.

9. Lora Wildenthal, *German Women for Empire, 1884–1945* (Durham: Duke University Press, 2001), 91.

10. Wildenthal, 135.

11. Wildenthal, 139.

12. Wildenthal, 163.

13. See Margaret Strobel and Nupur Chaudhuri, *Western Women and Imperialism: Complicity and Resistance* (Bloomington: Indiana University Press, 1992).

14. Lorcin, Introduction.

15. For Algerian case, see Lorcin, 22–23, 50–53.

16. Weitz, "Before the Holocaust."

17. For an overview, see Kevin Passmore, *Fascism: A Very Short Introduction* (Oxford: Oxford University Press, 2002). See also Mouton, *Nurturing the Nation.*

18. Benito Mussolini with Giovanni Gentile, "What is Fascism, 1932," Modern History Sourcebook, accessed December 2, 2011, http://www.fordham.edu/halsall/mod/mussolini-fascism.html.

19. Victoria de Grazia, *How Fascism Ruled Women: Italy, 1920–1945* (Berkeley and Los Angeles: University of California Press, 1992), 55.

20. De Grazia, 77–78.

21. "The 25 Points of 1920: An Early Nazi Program," Modern History Sourcebook, accessed October 1, 2011, http://www.fordham.edu/halsall/mod/25points.html.

22. For a discussion, see William H. Tucker, *The Science and Politics of Racial Research* (Champaign-Urbana: University of Illinois Press, 1996), 112–18.

23. Law for the Prevention of Offspring with Hereditary Diseases (July 14, 1933), in US Chief Counsel for the Prosecution of Axis Criminality, *Nazi Conspiracy and Aggression*, Vol. 5, Washington, DC: United States Government Printing Office, 1946, 3, Document 3067-PS, pp. 880–83, cited at German Historical Institute, German History in Documents and Images at http://germanhistorydocs.ghi-dc.org/pdf/eng/English30.pdf.

24. Robert Proctor, *Racial Hygiene: Medicine under the Nazis* (Cambridge, MA: Harvard University Press), 96.

25. Stefan Kühl, *The Nazi Connection: Eugenics, American Racism, and German National Socialism* (New York: Oxford University Press, 2002), 36.

26. Kühl, 90, 130.

27. Anita Harris, *Broken Patterns: Professional Women and the Quest for a New Feminine Identity* (Detroit: Wayne State University Press, 1995), 72–76.

28. This argument is fully developed in Elaine Tyler May, *Homeward Bound: American Families in the Cold War Era* (New York: Basic Books, 1988).

29. Mary N. Hampton, "Reaching Critical Mass? German Women and the 1998 Election," in David B. Conradt et al., *Power Shift in Germany: The 1998 Election and the End of the Kohl Era* (New York: Berghahn, 2000), 170.

30. See Agnes Joester and Insa Schöningh, eds., *So nah beieinander und doch so fern: Frauenleben in Ost und West* (Pfaffenweiler: Centaurus, 1992). Antje Reinheckel, Kornelia Franke, Wolfgang Weise, and Bernt-Peter Robra, "Effect of Re-Unification on Fertility Behaviour in East Germany: A Review of the Evidence," *Reproductive Health Matters* 6 (1998): 122–28.

31. Katherine Elizabeth Nash, "GDR Women and German Unification: Meanings of Paid Work and Child Care," (PhD diss., University of Minnesota, 1997), 94.

32. Reinheckel et al, 122–28.

33. Elizabeth Rosenthal, "Rural Flouting of One-Child Policy Undercuts China's Census," *New York Times*, April 14, 2000.

34. V. H. Thakor and Vinod M. Patel, "The Gujarat State Massive Vasectomy Campaign," *Studies in Family Planning*, 8 (1972): 188.

35. *The Economist*, February 11, 1999.

36. David G. Marr, *Vietnamese Tradition on Trial, 1920–1945* (Berkeley: University of California Press, 1981), 206.

37. Marr, 210.

38. Nguyen Van Luyen, "San Duc Chi-Nam" [Guide to Childbirth] (Hanoi, 1925). Cited and translated in Marr, 213.

39. Susan Bayly, *Asian Voices in a Postcolonial Age: Vietnam, India and Beyond* (Cambridge: Cambridge University Press, 2007), 64. Bayly is paraphrasing Ho.

40. *Nhung loi keu goi cua Ho Chu Tich* [The Appeals of President Ho] (Hanoi: Su That, 1958), 20–21. Cited and translated in Hue-Tam Ho Tai, *Radicalism and the Origins of the Vietnamese Revolution* (Cambridge, MA: Harvard University Press, 1992), 256–57.

41. Duong Van Mai Elliott, *The Sacred Willow: Four Generations of Life in a Vietnamese Family* (New York: Oxford University Press, 1999), 414.

42. There is a discussion of the iconic nature of the image in Bayly, 39.

43. The figures come from the General Office of Population and Family Planning: "Vietnam Population Quality Low, Warns Official," Baomi.com, August 21, 2009, accessed March 17, 2011, http://en.baomoi.com/Info/Vietnam-population-quality-low-warns-official/2/1412.epi.

44. H. T. Hoa et al., "Child Spacing and Two Child Policy in Practice in Rural Vietnam: Cross Sectional Survey," *BMJ* (1996) 313: 1113, accessed March 17, 2011, http://www.bmj.com/content/313/7065/1113.full.

45. "Vietnam Population Quality Low, Warns Official," accessed March 17, 2011.

EPILOGUE

1. From the collection "Digitizing Immigrant Letters" at the University of Minnesota Immigration History Research Center, http://www.ihrc.umn.edu/research/dil/Paikens/paikens.htm.

2. Carl Matthes, "South Africa: A Model for the Future," *LA Progressive*, February 5, 2010, http: //www.laproglessive.com/south-africa-model-future. Accessed February 24, 2012.

3. The amicus brief is available through the website of the American Historical Association, accessed October 1, 2011, http://www.historians.org/Perspectives/issues/2010/1011/2002-11-08-goodridge-amicus-history.pdf.

4. "Quaker Group Stops Certifying Marriages until Gay Marriage Legal," Minnesota Public Radio News, posted December 7, 2009, accessed October 3, 2011, http://minnesota.publicradio.org/display/web/2009/12/07/quaker-marriage/?refid=0.

5. Stephanie Saul, "Building a Baby, With Few Ground Rules," *New York Times*, December 13, 2009.

6. Ibid.

7. Judith Woods, "Careers Caught in a Club Sandwich," *Daily Telegraph*, December 9, 2009.

Further Reading

CHAPTER 1: Domestic Life and Human Origins (to 5000 BCE)

Cook, Michael. *A Brief History of the Human Race*. New York: W.W. Norton, 2003.

Gamble, Clive. *Origins and Revolutions: Human Identity in Earliest Prehistory*. Cambridge: Cambridge University Press, 2007.

Smail, Daniel Lord. *On Deep History and the Brain*. Berkeley: University of California Press, 2008.

Tattersall, Ian. *The World from Beginnings to 4000 BCE*. New York: Oxford University Press, 2008.

CHAPTER 2: The Birth of the Gods: Family in the Emergence of Religions (to 1000 ce)

Ahmed, Leila. *Women and Gender in Islam: Historical Roots of a Modern Debate*. New Haven: Yale University Press, 1992.

Brown, Peter. *Men, Women, and Sexual Renunciation in Early Christianity*. New York: Columbia University Press, 1988.

Doniger, Wendy. *The Hindus: An Alternative History*. New York: Penguin, 2009.

Lerner, Gerda. *The Creation of Patriarchy*. New York: Oxford University Press, 1986.

Paul, Diana. *Women in Buddhism: Images of the Feminine in the Mahayana Tradition*. Berkeley: University of California Press, 1985.

Raphals, Lisa. *Sharing the Light: Women and Virtue in Early China*. Albany: State University of New York Press, 1998.

CHAPTER 3: Ruling Families: Kinship at the Dawn of Politics (ca. 3000 BCE to 1450 CE)

Ardren, Traci, ed. *Ancient Maya Women*. Walnut Creek, CA: Altamira, 2002.

Bradley, Keith R. *Discovering the Roman Family: Studies in Roman Social History*. New York: Oxford University Press, 1991.

Nelson, Sarah Milledge, ed. *Ancient Queens: Archaeological Explorations*. Lanham, MD: Altamira, 2003.

Polgreen, Lydia. "Timbuktu Hopes Ancient Texts Spark a Revival," *New York Times*, August 7, 2007.

Pomeroy, Sarah. *Goddesses, Whores, Wives, and Slaves*. New York: Schocken, 1995.

Roller, Duane W. *Cleopatra: A Biography*. New York: Oxford University Press, 2010.

Watterson, Barbara. *Women in Ancient Egypt*. New York: St. Martin's, 1991.

CHAPTER 4: Early Modern Families (1400–1750)

Ebrey, Patricia. *The Inner Quarters: Marriage and the Lives of Chinese Women in the Sung Period*. Berkeley: University of California Press, 1993.

Herlihy, David. *Tuscans and their Families*. New Haven: Yale University Press, 1985.

Kinney, Anne Behnke, ed. *Chinese Views of Childhood*. Honolulu: University of Hawai'i Press, 1995.

Lal, Ruby. *Domesticity and Power in the Early Mughal World*. New York: Cambridge University Press, 2005.

Ozment, Steven E. *Three Behaim Boys Growing Up in Early Modern Germany: A Chronicle of Their Lives*. New Haven: Yale University Press, 1990.

Roper, Lyndal. "Luther: Sex, Marriage, and Motherhood," *History Today* 33:12 (December 1983): 33.

Seed, Patricia. *To Love, Honor, and Obey in Colonial Mexico: Marriage Choice 1574–1821*. Stanford, CA: Stanford University Press, 1992.

Wiesner-Hanks, Merry. *Women and Gender in Early Modern Europe*. 2nd ed. New York: Cambridge University Press, 2000.

CHAPTER 5: Families in Global Markets (1600–1850)

Blussé, Leonard. *Bitter Bonds: A Colonial Divorce Drama of the Seventeenth Century*. Princeton, NJ: M. Wiener, 2005.

Colley, Linda. *The Ordeal of Elizabeth Marsh: A Woman in World History*. New York: Pantheon, 2007.

Davis, Natalie Zemon. *The Return of Martin Guerre*. Cambridge: Harvard University Press, 1984.

González, Ondina E., and Bianco Premo, eds. *Raising an Empire: Children in Early Modern Iberia and Colonial Latin America*. Albuquerque: University of New Mexico Press, 2007.

Hecht, Tobias. ed., *Minor Omissions: Children in Latin American History and Society*. Madison: University of Wisconsin Press, 2002.

Mann, Susan. *Precious Records: Women in China's Long Eighteenth Century*. Stanford, CA: Stanford University Press, 1997.

O'Connor, Kaori. "The King's Christmas Pudding: Globalization, Recipes, and the Empire of Commodities," *Journal of Global History* 4 (2009): 127–55.

Reid, Anthony. *Southeast Asia in the Age of Commerce 1450–1800*. 2 vols. New Haven: Yale University Press, 1988.

Roth, Cecil. *Dona Gracia of the House of Nasi*. Philadelphia: Jewish Publication Society, 2009.

Studnicki-Gizbert, Daviken. *A Nation upon the Ocean Sea: Portugal's Atlantic Diaspora and the Crisis of Spanish Empire, 1492–1640*. New York: Oxford University Press, 2007.

CHAPTER 6: Families in Revolutionary Times (1750–1920)

Allen, Ann Taylor. *Feminism and Motherhood in Western Europe, 1890–1970: The Maternal Dilemma*. New York: Palgrave, 2007.

Desan, Suzanne. *The Family on Trial in Revolutionary France*. Berkeley: University of California Press, 2004.

Fernsebner, Susan. "A People's Playthings: Toys, Childhood and Chinese Identity, 1909–33," *Postcolonial Studies* 6:2 (2003), 269–93.

Glosser, Susan. *Chinese Visions of Family and State, 1915–1953*. Berkeley: University of California Press, 2003.

Hamlin, David. *Work and Play: The Production and Consumption of Toys in Germany, 1870–1914*. Ann Arbor: University of Michigan Press, 2007.

Honig, Emily. *Sisters and Strangers: Women in the Shanghai Cotton Mills*. Stanford, CA: Stanford University Press, 1992.

Jacobs, Harriet A. *Incidents in the Life of a Slave Girl: Written by Herself*. Edited by Jennifer Fleischner. Boston: Bedford/St. Martin's, 2010.

Kertzer, David, and Marzio Barbagli. *Family Life in the Long Nineteenth Century, 1789–1913*. New Haven: Yale University Press, 2002.

Mann, Susan. *The Talented Women of the Zhang Family*. Berkeley: University of California Press, 2007.

Maynes, Mary Jo. *Taking the Hard Road: Life Course in French and German Workers' Autobiographies in the Era of Industrialization*. Chapel Hill: University of North Carolina Press, 1995.

Popp, Adelheid. *The Autobiography of a Working Woman*. Chicago: T.G. Browne, 1913.

Pruitt, Ida. *The Daughter of Han: The Autobiography of a Chinese Working Woman*. 1945. Reprint, Eastford, CT: Martino Fine Books, 2011.

Smith, Bonnie G. *Ladies of the Leisure Class: The Bourgeoises of Northern France in the Nineteenth Century*. Princeton, NJ: Princeton University Press, 1981.

CHAPTER 7: Powers of Life and Death: Families in the Era of State Population Management (1880 to the Present)

Bayly, Susan. "Narrating Family Lives in Present-day Hanoi," in *Asian Voices in a Postcolonial Age: Vietnam, India and Beyond*. Cambridge: Cambridge University Press, 2007.

Clancy-Smith, Julia, and Frances Gouda, eds. *Domesticating the Empire: Languages of Gender, Race and Family Life in French and Dutch Colonialism*. Charlottesville: University Press of Virginia, 1998.

de Grazia, Victoria. *How Fascism Ruled Women: Italy, 1920–1945*. Berkeley: University of California Press, 1992.

May, Elaine Tyler. *Homeward Bound: American Families in the Cold War Era*. New York: Basic Books, 1988.

Meriwether, Margaret, and Judith E. Tucker, eds. *Social History of Women and Gender in the Modern Middle East*. Boulder, CO: Westview, 1999.

The Modern Girl around the World Research Group, *The Modern Girl around the World: Consumption, Modernity and Globalization*. Durham, NC: Duke University Press, 2008.

Mouton, Michelle. *From Nurturing the Nation to Purifying the Volk: Weimar and Nazi Family Policy, 1918–1945*. Princeton, NJ: Princeton University Press, 2009.

Strobel, Margaret, and Nupur Chaudhuri, eds. *Western Women and Imperialism: Complicity and Resistance*. Bloomington: Indiana University Press, 1992.

Thompson, Elizabeth. *Colonial Citizens: Republican Rights, Paternal Privilege, and Gender in French Syria and Lebanon*. New York: Columbia University Press, 2000.

White, Tyrene. *China's Longest Campaign: Birth Planning in the People's Republic of China*. Ithaca, NY: Cornell University Press. 2006.

Wildenthal, Lora. *German Women for Empire, 1884–1945*. Durham, NC: Duke University Press, 2001.

Websites

America from the Great Depression to WWII: Photographs from the FSA-OWI 1935–1945
http://lcweb2.loc.gov/ammem/fsahtml/fahome.html
This site houses 160,000 photographs of the Farm Security Administration–Office of War Information Collection of the Library of Congress. The keyword-searchable images show Americans at home, at work, and at play, with an emphasis on rural and small-town life and the adverse effects of the Great Depression, the Dust Bowl, and increasing farm mechanization.

Children & Youth in History
http://chnm.gmu.edu/cyh/
A world history resource that provides teachers and students with access to primary sources about young people from the past to the present. Created by the Roy Rosenzweig Center for History and New Media at George Mason University and the University of Missouri-Kansas City.

Coming of Age in Ancient Greece
http://hoodmuseum.dartmouth.edu/exhibitions/coa/
This site, from the Hood Museum of Art at Dartmouth College, includes quotations from Greek authors about children and also some exemplary stele (grave) images that memorialize children who have died.

German History in Documents and Images
http://germanhistorydocs.ghi-dc.org/index.cfm
This bilingual site, developed by the German Historical Institute in Washington, D.C., archives essays, images, and translated documents relating to many aspects of German history, including family life.

Heilbrunn Timeline of Art History
http://www.metmuseum.org/toah/
Developed by the Metropolitan Museum of Art, this site includes images and essays on artistic representations of many aspects of world history, organized by time period and region.

Liberty, Equality, Fraternity: Exploring the French Revolution
http://chnm.gmu.edu/revolution/
This site, developed as a collaboration of the Roy Rosenzweig Center for History and New Media (George Mason University) and the American Social History Project (City University of New York), houses more than 600 documents and sources related to the era of the French Revolution, including sources about gender and family relations.

The National Museum of American Jewish History
http://www.nmajh.org/collection.aspx
The museum's site offers access to digitized images and stories relating to family life as well as other aspects of American Jewish life submitted by museum visitors.

A Visual Sourcebook of Chinese Civilization
http://depts.washington.edu/chinaciv/timeline.htm
This website, prepared by Patricia Buckley Ebrey, has images, maps, and information about daily life in Chinese history.

Visualizing China
http://visualisingchina.net/
This site, developed by the Department of Historical Studies at the University of Bristol, has more than 8,000 keyword-searchable digitized images of historical photographs of China taken between 1850 and 1950, including hundreds of photos of families, children, and homes.

Women in World History
http://chnm.gmu.edu/wwh/sources.php
A project of the Roy Rosenzweig Center for History and New Media at George Mason University, this site provides access to sources about women throughout the world. Women in World History is a project of the Roy Rosenzweig Center for History and New Media, George Mason University, and part of World History Matters

The World Digital Library
http://www.wdl.org/en/
This site, developed by the U.S. Library of Congress and UNESCO, makes available in multilingual format significant primary materials, especially images, from countries and cultures around the world; viewers can search by time period or region.

Ying Yu Tang: A Chinese Home
http://www.pem.org/sites/yinyutang/
Developed by the Peabody Essex Museum, this site depicts a multigeneration home from China and explores the history of the family that lived in it.

Acknowledgments

Writing this book took us into many unfamiliar arenas of scholarship. We are most appreciative for all of the advice along the way from colleagues at the University of Minnesota and beyond. These colleagues have saved us from errors and misunderstandings, but we cannot hold them responsible for the ones that remain. The ideas for this book emerged from many years of teaching world history at Minnesota. Thanks are due to the many talented teaching assistants from all areas of history who worked with us on that course. We refined our ideas in our first offering of a new course, "The History of the Family from 10,000 BCE to the Present," in 2009, and we offer thanks to the students in that class, and especially to the two TAs, Qin Fang and Emily Bruce. Earlier versions of chapters were presented at our department's Workshop for the Comparative History of Women, Gender, and Sexuality, at the Social Science History Association meeting, and at meetings of the World History Association. We want to thank panel members, commentators, and audiences at those sessions for their helpful feedback. In addition we want to thank David Good, Patrick McNamara, Derek Peterson, and Eva von Dassow for close and helpful readings of various drafts. We also want to thank the editorial staff at Oxford University Press, in particular Nancy Toff and Sonia Tycko, for their encouragement, advice, and support throughout the writing process, as well as the anonymous reviewers who gave us helpful feedback on our manuscript draft. Last but not least, we want to thank Nancy and Dave Huisenga, innkeepers at the Habberstad House Bed and Breakfast in Lanesboro, Minnesota, for their warm hospitality and logistical support during three periods of intensive writing that were crucial for the completion of this book.

Index

Page numbers written in **bold** denote photographs or illustrations.

Catholicism
  control over family life and marriage, 57
  Council of Trent, 57, 58
  elevation of celibacy over marriage, 55
  imposition in Mexico, 49, 52, 54, 58
  Protestant Reformation, 54–57, 84
Caucasus, 33
Chen, Duxiu, 92
childbearing. *See* reproduction
childcare
  in East and West Germany, 108–10
  as state policy, 96, **108**, 110
child labor, in industrial revolution, 80, 81–82,
    83, 84
children
  adoption policies, 119, 120–21
  in Aranda culture, 20
  in Athenian culture, 43–44
  and Chinese filial piety, 40, 91, 112
  of Chinese merchant families, 70, 71
  Chinese one-child policy, 110–11, **111**, 115,
    122
  in colonial Africa, 98, 100
  as commodities, 120
  in early civilization, 1, 5, 9, 10, 12–13
  Enlightenment gender expectations, 85–86
  of Islamic slaves, 75
  as laborers in industrial revolution, 80,
    81–82, 83, 84
  in Mayan culture, 41
  Mexican mixed race, 58, **60**
  in Nazi Germany, 103, **104**
  in post-Napoleonic France, 89
  in revolutionary China, 94
  under Catholic Church, 57–58
  under Code of Hammurabi, 31–32
  under Islam, 23
  of U.S. slaves, 73, 74
  See also childcare; reproduction
China (modern)
  desire for modern goods, 92–94
  elder care, 122
  industrialization, 89
  local products movements, 92, 94
  May Fourth Movement, 92
  one-child policy, 110–11, **111**, 115, 122
  patrilineal system, 110
  reform and revolution, 89–92
  See also revolutions
China (premodern)
  ancestor veneration, 11–12
  burial practices, 15
  dynastic transmission of power, 38–39, 41,
    43
  family metaphors in conceptualization of
    rule, 39–40
  global trade in early modern era, 70–72, **72**
  hereditary kingship, 41, 43
  introduction of Buddhism, 27

patriliny, 39, 43
  role of merit in political power, 38–39,
    40
  See also Confucianism; Yangshao culture
Christianity
  emergence of, **24**, 28
  origin stories, 17, 19
  roots of monotheism, 19–20
  views of women and family life, 28–29
  See also Catholicism
Christmas Carol, A (Dickens), 63
civilization, early
  agriculture, 4–5, **6–7**, 8, 10
  animal domestication, 4, 5, 10, 13
  crop domestication, 4–5, **6–7**, 13
  different types of, 13
  divisions of labor in, 3, 4, 5, 8
  fertility figures, 1, **2**
  food acquisition, 3–8
  modes of subsistence, 4
  religious beliefs, 15–16
  ritual objects, 14–15
  role of kin groups, 3–5, 8–13
  settlements, 5, 8–13
  sites of, **6–7**
  theories of gender, 1–3, 10–11, 12, 33
  See also ancestor veneration; archaeology;
    burial practices; Caral; Çatalhöyük;
    Paloma; religion; Yangshao culture
Cixi, Empress, 89
class and family life
  caste system in India, 20–21
  in classical Athens, 43
  during industrial revolution, 80–84, **86**
  and food acquisition in early modern Europe,
    64
  in Mesopotamia, 31
  in Mexico, 58–59, **60**, 62
  in revolutionary China, 91, 94
  in Timbuktu, 46–47
  welfare recipients, 96, 105
Code of Hammurabi, 32
Cold War era, 107–08, 113
colonial rule
  in Algeria, 97, 99–100
  citizenship issues, 100
  family metaphors in, 97
  in French West Africa, 97, 99, 100
  in German East Africa, 100
  in German Southwest Africa, 98–99, 100
  in Kenya, 111–12
  as key to European population management,
    96–97
  racialist policies in, 100
  relationships with indigenous populations,
    97–99
  in Vietnam, 112–13, 115
  See also Mexico (early modern era)
Columbus, Christopher, 49, 51, 54, 61

Confucianism
  on filial piety, 40, 92, 112, 113
  on Five Relationships, 40
  origins of, **25**, 39
  patriarchal authority of, 40, 71, 92
  role in historic events, 92, 112, 113
contraception, 96, 107, 110, 121
Costa, Alexander da, 67
Costa, Benjamin da, 68
Costa de León, Abram da, 67–68
Costa family, 67–68, 72
cotton production, 81–82
Council of Trent, 57, 58
creation stories. *See* origin stories

deep history
  chronology of world events, 123–24
  defined, xiii
Dickens, Charles, 63
division of labor
  in contemporary society, 121–22
  in early civilization, 3, 4, 5, 8
  in industrial revolution, 81–82, **83**
  in modern China, 90–91
  in post-war East and West Germany, 108–09
  in Yangshao culture, 10–11, 13
  See also gender
domestication
  animal, 4, 5, 10, 13
  crop, 4–5, **6–7**, 13
  See also agriculture
Doppelmayr, Friedrich Wilhelm, **86**
Duong, Quoc Trong, 114
dynasties. *See* emperors; kingships; politics

early modern era
  shaped by family life, 62
  See also families, early modern; Mexico (early modern era); religion; trade
East Africa (early civilization)
  cross-marriages, 8
  division of labor, 3
  food acquisition, 3, 8
  human origins in, 3
  See also civilization, early
East Africa (early modern era)
  political authority, 69
  slave trade, 74–75
  trade relationships in, 69, 72
East Africa (German), 100
East Germany, 107–10, 115
Eberhardt, Isabelle, 99
Egypt (ancient)
  agriculture, 5, 16
  burial practices, 15
  female kings, 36–37
  female political and personal power, 33, 36–38
  Greek conquerors, 33, 36
  kingships, 36–38, 41, 43

legal codes, 36
  origin stories, 16–17, **18, 24**
  role of kinship in transmission of power, 36–38, 41, 43
  sibling marriages, 16, 36, 43
elder care, 121–22
Emile (Rousseau), 85, 88
emperors
  Chinese dynastic, 38–40, 41, 44–45, 47–48, 89–90
  Mughal, 52
  Napoleon as self-proclaimed, 88–89
  See also specific emperors
Engels, Friedrich, 82–83
Enkheduanna, 31
Enlightenment, 84–88
eugenics, 103–04, 105, 112
Eumenides (Aeschylus), 44
Europe
  agricultural trade in early modern era, 63–64
  community oversight of sexuality and marriage, 76–79, **77**
  dynastic monarchies, 84
  early modern farming traditions, 75–79
  first millennium BCE burial sites, 15–16
  industrial revolution, 82–84, 89, 91
  notions of hereditary rule in, 54
  Protestant Reformation, 54–57, 84
  putting-out industries, 77–78
  regulation of surrogacy, 120
  See also colonial rule; state population management
Eve, 19, 29

families
  as agents of historical transformation, xi–xii, xiii
  chronology, 123–24
  definition of, xii–xiii
  as historical construction, xi
  placing at center of history, xi
  See also families, early modern; families of the future; food and family life; migrations; religion; revolutions (1750–1920); trade
families, early modern
  encounters between Old World and New, 49
  increase in cross-cultural understandings, 50–51
  renegotiation of family rituals, 49
  See also Mexico (early modern era); migrations; trade
families of the future
  adoptions, 119, 120–21
  elder care, 121–22
  family ties across distance, 117–18
  gay rights movement, 118–19
  reproductive health care, 121
  reproductive technologies, 119–20

fascism, 100–101, 102, 105
  See also Nazi Germany
female circumcision, 112
Ferdinand, King, 54, 61
Fertile Crescent, agriculture in, 4
First Indochina War, 113
food and family life
  in ancient Turkey, 50
  in Chinese merchant families, 71
  in early human civilization, 3–8, 9,
    10, 13
  in Mesopotamia, 31
  new ideas under Lutheran reform, **56**
  New World crops in early modern Europe,
    63–64
  welfare recipients, 96, 105
  See also agriculture
France
  colonial Vietnam, 112–13, 115
  French Revolution, 84–88
  reproductive health care, 121
French Revolution, 84–88
Friends (Quakers), 119
future of families. *See* families of the future

gay rights movement, 118–19
  See also homosexuality
gender
  in burial practices, 11, 15–16
  in colonial Africa, 97, 99
  disadvantaging of women in early
    civilizations, 33, 36, 43
  Enlightenment ideals of, 85–88
  norms in East and West Germany, 108–10
  theories of early civilization, 1–3, 10–11, 12,
    33
  See also division of labor; emperors;
    kingships; marriage; matriarchal societies;
    patriarchy; queens
Genesis, creation story, 17, 19
German Democratic Republic (East Germany),
  107–08
German Empire
  family-based systems of trade and
    government, 47
  health insurance in 19th century, 96
  role of wealth in political power, 47
  See also Protestant Reformation
Germany
  post-WWII division of, 107–08
  See also East Africa (German); East Germany;
    Nazi Germany; Southwest Africa
    (German); West Germany
Ghana
  ancient, **34**, 44
  modern, 5
Goodridge v. Department of Public Health,
  119
Gouges, Olympe de, 87, 88

Great Britain
  contemporary families, 121–22
  industrial revolution, 81–83, 89
  working-class mothers, 96
Great Depression, 105
Greece (ancient)
  male authority over women, 28, 33,
    36, 43
  patrilineal culture, 23, 43–44
Guangxu, Emperor of China, 89

Habsburg monarchy, 54
Hamburg, 47, 48
Han dynasty, 39, 40
Hanseatic League, 34
Harun al-Rashid, Caliph, 26
Hatshepsut, 36–37, **37**
Herero people, 100
Herodotus, 33
Hess, Rudolf, 103
Hinduism
  caste system, 26
  prescriptions for marriage, 20–22
  sacred texts, 20–21, **25**
Hitler, Adolf, 101–02, 103
  See also Nazi Germany
Ho, Chi Minh, 113
homosexuality
  and adoption politics, 120
  gay rights movement, 118–19
  under Italian fascism, 101
Horus, 16, **18**
hunter-gatherers, 3–4, 5
  See also civilization, early

Ibn Battuta, 50
Illinois excavations, 8
imperialism. *See* colonial rule
India
  arrival of Islam, 52
  caste system, 21
  modern population control, 111
  origins of agriculture, 4
  See also Akbar
Indian Ocean
  Chinese traders, 70
  slavery, 74–75
  See also East Africa
Industrial Revolution, 80–84, 89, 91
Isabella, Queen, 54, 61
Isis, 16–17, **18**
Islam
  centers of learning, 45–46
  in colonial Algeria, 97, 100
  marriage rules, 22–23, 26
  slavery laws, 74–75
  women's subservience to men, 19–20, 22–23,
    26, 97
  See also Muhammad; Ottoman Empire

Israelites
  patriliny, 19–20
  See also Jews and Judaism
Italy
  politicization of family, 101, **102**
  population management by, 100–101
  See also fascism

Jacobs, Harriet, 74
janissary system, 51–52
Java, 70–71, 72
Jews and Judaism
  in Nazi Germany, 102, 104, **106**
  patriarchal societies of, 19–20, 23, 28
  Sephardic Jewish diaspora, 65–69

Kay, Joseph, 81
Kenya, 111–12
Khadija, 22
Khrushchev, Nikita, 107
kingship
  ancient Egyptian, 36–38, 41, 43
  hereditary, 41, 43
  Mayan culture, 41, 43
  Mesopotamian, 30–32, 41, 43
  See also emperors; *specific kings*
kinship
  archaeological explorations of, 9–13
  definition of, xii
  See also children; families; kingships;
    marriage; politics; trade
Kintampo, 5, **6**, 8
Kitchen Debate, 107
Knight, Charles, 63

Landskroener, Paul, 119
Laws of Manu, 21–22
legal codes
  ancient Egyptian, 36
  ancient Hindu laws of marriage, 21–22
  apartheid laws of South Africa, 105
  Code of Hammurabi, 32
  Islamic laws on slaves, 74–75
  Mesopotamian, 31–32
  Napoleonic, 88–89
  Nazi sterilization laws, 95–96, 103–04, 105
  power of men in, 32
  U.S. sterilization laws, 105
Lenz, Fritz, 103
Leo Africanus, 45
Leutwein, Theodor, 98
Lilienkron, Ada von, 98
Louis XVI, King of France, 87
Lübeck, 47
Lutheran reform, 55–57, 84
Luther, Martin, 54–55, 57

Madonna (singer), 120
Mali Empire, **34**, 44

Marie Antoinette, Queen, 87
marriage
  Aranda rules, 20
  by Chinese merchants, 70–71, **72**
  in colonial Africa, 98–99
  in dynastic China, 39, 40, 45
  in early Christianity, 28–29
  in early civilization, 3, 8, 9, 10, 12
  in early Egypt, 16, 36, 43
  in early European agricultural communities,
    76–79, **77**
  in early modern China, 91
  in early modern East Africa, 69
  in European monarchies, 54
  gay, 118–19
  Hindu prescriptions for, 20–22
  in Industrial Revolution, 88
  Islamic rules for, 22–23, 26
  in Mayan culture, 41, 43
  in Mughal empire, 52, **53**
  in Nazi Germany, 103, 104, **106**
  in post-Napoleonic France, 88–89
  in post-reunification Vietnam, 114
  in post-war Germany, 108
  in Sephardic Jewish merchant families,
    65–66, **67**
  by slaves, 73
  in South Africa, 105
  under Catholicism, 55, 57–58
  under Lutheranism, 55, 57
  under Zoroastrianism, 23
  See also Mexico (early modern era)
Marshall, Margaret, 119
Marx, Karl, 82
Mathes, Carl, 118
matriarchal societies
  in ancient civilizations, 33
  in early human groups, 1
  in mythology, 33
matriliny, in Arabian Peninsula, 23
Mau-Mau, 112
Maya culture
  ancestor veneration, 41
  as early political state, **34**
  hereditary transmission of power, 40–41,
    42
  kingships, 41, 43
  origin stories and emergence of religion, 17,
    24
  patrilineal kinship systems, 41
  queens, 41, **42**
  role of kin connections, 41–43
Mendes, Beatrice, 65–66
Mendes, Diego, 65
Mesopotamia
  burial practices, 15
  family law codes, 31–32
  kingships, 30–32, 41, 43
  male-female balance of power, 31–32

Mesopotami (*continued*)
role of family in transmission of power, 30–31, **35**, 41, 43
Mexico (ancient)
burial practices, 15
See also Maya culture
Mexico (early modern era)
casta paintings, **60**, 61–62
imposition of Christianity, 49, 52, 54, 58
intermarriage and racial questions, 59–62
post-conquest marriage practices, 49, 58–59
pre-conquest marriage practices, 49, 58
Spanish conquest, 49, 52, 54
middle-class families
in industrial revolution, 82–84, **86**
in revolutionary China, 91
See also class and family life
migrations
in contemporary world, 117–18, 122
patterns in early human development, 3, 8
Sephardic Jewish diaspora, 65–69
of women to European colonies, 98–100
missionaries, 57, 112
Moctezuma, 58
monarchies. *See* politics
monotheism, 19
Montesquieu, Charles de Secondat, Baron, 84–85
Mu'awiyya, 44
Mughals, 52, **53**
Muhammad, 22–23
See also Islam
Mulian, 27
Mussolini, Benito, 101

Nama people, 100
Napoleon, dawn of, 88–89
Nazi Germany
biological and reproductive policies, 101–02
concentration camps, 104
glorification of ideal family, 103, **104**, 108, 115
Law for Prevention of Offspring with Hereditary Disease, 103–04
Law for the Encouragement of Marriage, 103
Marital Health Law, 104
Nuremberg Laws, 104, **106**
population management, 95–96
racialist policies, 102–04
sterilization laws, 95–96, 103–04, 105
Nefertiti, Queen, 37, **38**
Neolithic Revolution, 5
New Guinea, agriculture in, 4
New Julfa, 65
Nile Valley, 5, **35**
See also Egypt (ancient)
Nixon, Richard, 107
Norte Chico, 12
See also Caral
North Africa, 23, 44

North America
early agriculture, 6, 8
See also United States
Nuremberg Laws, 104, **106**
Nzinga Mbemba, 73

Old Testament, 19, **24**
Opium War, 89
origin stories
Biblical, 17, 19
Egyptian, 16–17, **18**, **24**
family relationships in, 14, 16–19
Mayan, 17, **24**
orphans, 120–21
Osiris, 16
Ottoman Empire, 51–52, 63

Pacal, 41, **42**
Paloma, 6, 12, 13
pastoralism, 3, 4
patriarchy
emergence of, 1, 19
and emergence of monotheism, 19
Enlightenment critique of, 84
patriliny, 19–20
peasant families
in early modern Europe, 76–79
See also class and family life
Persian Empire, 23
politics
dynastic empires, 32–43, 44–45, 47–48
in early civilization, 9, 10, 12–13, 47–48
Enlightenment theories of, 84–85
hereditary kingships, 41, 43
non-dynastic family rule, 43–48
role of kinship, xii, 30–33
role of military, 33
See also Athens (classical); China (modern); China (premodern); East Africa; Egypt (ancient); Maya culture; revolutions (1750–1920); state population management; Timbuktu
Popol Vuh, 17, **24**
population control. *See* state population management
Portugal, 52, 54, 61
preagricultural societies, 3
See also civilization, early
Protestant Reformation, 54–57, 84

Qin dynasty, 39
Qing dynasty, 89, 90, 110
queens
role in Egyptian power structures, 36, 37–38, 39, 43
role in Mayan power structures, 41, **42**
role of Chinese empresses, 39
See also specific queens
Qur'an, 22, **24**

race, conceptual development of, 59–62
Rahula, 26, 27
religion
  burial sites as clues to, 15–16
  early sites of, **24–25**
  emergence of monotheism, 19–20
  family as ideal site for, 14, 16–26, 29
  family in competition with, 26–29
  gay marriage debate, 118–19
  missionaries, 57, 112
  oldest ritual objects, 14–15
  origin stories, 14, 16–19
  prescriptions on family life, 14, 20
  prescriptions on marriage, 20–26
  See also Buddhism; Catholicism; Christianity;
    Hinduism; Islam; Jews and Judaism;
    Protestant Reformation; Zoroastrianism
reproduction
  contraception, 96, 107, 110, 121
  in early human civilization, 3
  health care, 121
  new technologies assisting, 119–20
  surrogacy, 119–20
  See also state population management
Revolutionary Army, The (Zou), 90
revolutions (1750–1920)
  Chinese family reforms, 91, 92
  Chinese industrialization, 89, 90–91, 92–94
  Chinese uprisings, 90, 92
  democratization of family life, 88
  European protoindustries, 80–81
  French Revolution, 84–88
  industrial, 82–84, 89, 91
  May Fourth Movement, 92
  reversals under Napoleon, 88–89
Rhodes, Cecil, 97
Roman Catholic Church. *See* Catholicism
Roman Empire
  cult of Isis, 17
  patriarchal beliefs, 23, 28
Rousseau, Jean-Jacques, 85–86, 88

Sachs, Hans, **56**
sacred texts
  Hindu, 20–21, **25**
  See also Bible; Qur'an
Sargon, King, 31
Scythia, 33
Sephardic Jewish diaspora, 65–69
sexuality
  and *casta* racial classifications, 59
  in colonial Africa, 97–99
  in early Christianity, 28–29
  in early civilization, 1, 3
  in European agricultural communities, 76–79, 77
  of slaves, 74
  as symbol of political power, 52
  under Lutheranism, 55

See also homosexuality; marriage
Shanghai, 91
Shun, 38–39
Siddhartha, 26–27
slaves and slavery
  family bonds in New World, 73–74, **75**
  on Indian Ocean plantations, 74–75
  loss of African family bonds, 64, 73
Social Contract, The (Rousseau), 85
Songhai Empire, **34**, 44
South Africa, 105, 118
South America, female warriors, 33
South Asia
  female warriors, 33
  See also India
Southwest Africa (German), 98–99, 100
Soviet Union, 106–08, 113
Spain
  interest in colonization, 52, 53
  political consolidation with Portugal,
    54, 61
  See also Mexico (early modern era)
Spirit of the Laws, The (Montesquieu),
    84–85
state population management
  Chinese one-child policy, 110–11, **111**, 115,
    122
  in East and West Germany, 107–10, 115
  eugenics movement, 103–04, 105, 112
  in European colonies, 96–100, 111–14, 115
  in India, 111
  in Nazi Germany, 95–96, 103–04, 105
  post-WWII, 107
  South African apartheid laws, 105
  under fascism, 100–101
  in United States, 105
  welfare measures, 105
  See also Nazi Germany
sterilization laws
  in Nazi Germany, 95–96, 103–04, 105
  in United States, 105
Stone Age, 5
sugar industry, 68
Sumer, 30
surrogacy, 119–20

Tarbo, 29
Tertullian, 29
Timbuktu, 45–47, 48
totem groups, 20
trade
  agricultural trade, 63–64, 71–72, 73, 74
  Armenian merchants and kinship networks,
    64–65, 69
  Chinese traders in Indian Ocean, 70–72, **72**
  East African traders, 69
  family transformations, 64
  impact on European farm traditions, 76–79
  role of kinship networks in, xii, 64, 71

The New Oxford World History

CHRONOLOGICAL VOLUMES

The World from Beginnings to 4000 BCE
The World from 4000 to 1000 BCE
The World from 1000 BCE to 500 CE
The World from 300 to 1000 CE
The World from 1000 to 1500
The World from 1450 to 1700
The World in the Eighteenth Century
The World in the Nineteenth Century
The World in the Twentieth Century

THEMATIC AND TOPICAL VOLUMES

The City: A World History
Democracy: A World History
Food: A World History
Empires: A World History
The Family: A World History
Genocide: A World History
Health and Medicine: A World History
Migration: A World History
Race: A World History
Technology: A World History

GEOGRAPHICAL VOLUMES

The Atlantic in World History
Central Asia in World History
China in World History
Japan in World History
Mexico in World History
Russia in World History
The Silk Road in World History
South Africa in World History
South Asia in World History
Southeast Asia in World History
Trans-Saharan Africa in World History